02/23/21

Enjoy the story!

Many Blessings,

48

An Experiential Memoir on Homelessness

Dr. Sheldon A. Jacobs

This book is a work of non-fiction. Unless otherwise noted, the author and the publisher make no explicit guarantees as to the accuracy of the information contained in this book and in some cases, names of people and places have been altered to protect their privacy.

Archway Publishing books may be ordered through booksellers or by contacting:

Archway Publishing
1663 Liberty Drive
Bloomington, IN 47403
www.archwaypublishing.com
844-669-3957

Because of the dynamic nature of the Internet, any web addresses or links contained in this book may have changed since publication and may no longer be valid. The views expressed in this work are solely those of the author and do not necessarily reflect the views of the publisher, and the publisher hereby disclaims any responsibility for them.

Any people depicted in stock imagery provided by Getty Images are models, and such images are being used for illustrative purposes only.
Certain stock imagery © Getty Images.

Interior Image Credit: Benjamin Hager/Las Vegas Review-Journal

Scripture quotations are from the ESV® Bible (The Holy Bible, English Standard Version®), copyright © 2001 by Crossway, a publishing ministry of Good News Publishers. Used by permission. All rights reserved.

ISBN: 978-1-4808-9623-9 (sc)
ISBN: 978-1-4808-9624-6 (hc)
ISBN: 978-1-4808-9625-3 (e)

Library of Congress Control Number: 2020917947

Print information available on the last page.

Archway Publishing rev. date: 10/30/2020

To the lady from the gym who inspired me beyond anything I could ever imagine, to move forward with living on the streets for forty-eight hours, to provide hope to the hopeless, lend a voice to the voiceless, and shine light when there is so much dark.

CONTENTS

PREFACE

Whoever gives to the poor will not want, but he who hides his eyes will get many a curse.
                                        —Proverbs 28:27 (ESV)

I don't know what will come from sharing my homeless experience with the world. In fact, I don't even know if this memoir will even move the needle. I'm fully aware of all the complexities surrounding homelessness, and my only hope, prayer, wish, want, and request is that my experience somehow inspires some sort of change pertaining to this social ill. And if change does not occur, all is well because I have already been greatly affected by this experience. I learned one main truth, and that is homelessness can affect anyone. It does not matter how much money you once had, which part of the sociocultural strata you fall on, how large your family is, what color your skin is, or what your political party is. Anyone can be homeless. I also learned that surviving on the streets is very hard. The physical and mental toll that it takes on you is enough to make cigarettes, drugs, alcohol, and denial seem like the only available coping methods.

Many will criticize me for only living two days instead of two weeks or two months on the streets. They may say two days is not enough to provide an accurate portrayal of what it is truly like to be homeless. And that is completely fine. I have learned that you can't please everyone. I will say that a lot of folks outside of this project who have experienced some form of homelessness in their lives have commended me for what I have done because I went out of my way to understand something that many are either unable to or simply refuse to understand. Even though it was only forty-eight hours, every minute of my experience was excruciating. I went from being a successful, middle-class family man one day to being without food, money, shelter, and technology the very same night. The mental toll alone was the greatest challenge I have ever experienced. Not being able to sleep comfortably due to the hardness of the concrete and having to essentially sleep with one eye open were tough.

The undesirable pain I experienced long after I completed the forty-eight-hour journey is still with me to this very day. The way people from the outside world looked down at me, stared past me, or did not look at me at all remains with me. I had never felt so low in my life. On top of that, I left my family, especially my wife, wondering if she would ever see me again. So, it might have been only forty-eight hours, but those forty-eight hours felt like forty-eight days.

What frustrates me the most about homelessness is people who hold positions to facilitate change but instead cowardly run behind the narrative that homeless people have made a choice to be homeless. Folks from across our nation—policy makers, colleagues, family members, friends, neighbors, and community leaders—truly refuse to help. In fact, several days after I completed my forty-eight hours, I was involved in a heated discussion with a colleague who said, "If so many people don't want to be homeless, then why are there so many homeless across the globe?" That was the basis of why this person thought being homeless was strictly a choice, and the person who made this statement is well educated and well informed, which only shows that there are a lot of people who share the same sentiments toward the homeless.

So how does someone end up homeless? This is certainly a

loaded question, but the question was always in the back of my mind when I befriended homeless individuals during my experience. The reality was that it is easy for a person to end up homeless—and it is much harder for most people who are homeless to no longer be homeless. Thus, if it is that easy for a good portion of people in any community to end up being homeless, and that much harder for the majority of those people who are homeless to get back on their feet, then that means you will always have people who end up homeless and even more people who struggle to find their footing. I feel that homelessness is a problem that will never completely go away, but I am hopeful that one day homelessness will no longer be a crisis but a problem that is able to be effectively managed. I believe we can get there as long as we collectively learn as much as we can about the problem that we are trying to solve.

As I mentioned earlier, my forty-eight-hour experience was the most challenging endeavor I ever faced. I think that if I remained on the streets beyond the forty-eight hours, I would have hit a breaking point. I was increasingly feeling helpless, and the only thing that got me through was knowing that there was light among all the darkness. I knew that if I stayed out of harm's way, I would be going home to see my family. However, what about the thousands across the globe who are truly homeless? For many, it's a temporary shortcoming that can be overcome. For many others, it's a twenty-foot dark hole with virtually no way out. Just when you find a small crevice or two to support your footing, you climb your way up, only to find out that the crevice is not strong enough to support you. You fall right back down to where you were—at the bottom of the dark hole. So many people I met during this journey shared these sentiments, but surprisingly, they also seemed to understand there is light in the midst of the darkness. What makes light thrive is its ability to expose darkness. With light, we can cling to hope—and it is that hope that can set us free.

ACKNOWLEDGMENTS

To my Lord and Savior, Jesus Christ. To my parents, Vernetta Stewart, Darryl Jacobs, and Edwin Steverson; to my grandparents, Winfred and Ethel Stewart; and my wife, Nicole, you have all been an inspiration to my success. Also, to my children, Jayden and Arianna; my siblings, Tammy, Darryl Jr., Adrien, Lauren, Myla, Kenny, Carla, Erica, and Jennifer; and to the many who have touched me in some way, shape, or form.

Many thanks to all the individuals I came across during my time on the streets. I did my best to recreate your stories as you told them, and I also changed your names as well as the names of the places I frequented to maintain anonymity. All of you embraced me and took me in during my forty-eight hours, thank you. I likely would not have made it through without your support, wisdom, humor, sadness, despair, hope, mistrust, frustration, curiosity, anger, sickness, kindness, and generosity. I took away these themes from your journeys that you courageously shared with me, a total stranger. It was your collective journeys that gave me the additional strength to get through the weekend of August 30, 2018, through September 2, 2018. Those forty-eight hours were by far the hardest thing I ever had to endure in my lifetime. I will never look at someone experiencing homelessness the same ever again. So, thank you! In the same breath, I apologize for not being authentic with you. I was trying to experience homelessness in its purest form, and I knew that if I shared with you who I really was, I would have lost all credibility.

A burden I still carry with me to this day is that, after those forty-eight hours, my life returned to normal. I was able to return to my two-story house in the suburbs to be with my wife and kids. Most, if not all, of you did not have that option of going home to something better. There was a part of me that felt guilty, like I was leaving you behind, which is probably a regular struggle you experience with humanity. I felt what you felt even though it was only for a short time. It was real though. It was something that nobody from the outside could ever understand unless he or she has lived it. So, I hope you can forgive me, as I did not mean any harm.

Last but not least, I must dedicate this to the life of Ethel Stewart, whose selflessness for the marginalized left a fire in me. I will graciously carry the torch you left, Nana, and right before it's my time to see you again, I will eagerly pass the torch to someone else.

INTRODUCTION

Every day, when I drove through downtown Las Vegas and saw the droves of homeless people doing all they could to survive the harsh summers and the cold winters of the Mojave Desert, I often wondered what I could do to help them. I simply did not know how, which left me feeling hopeless. As a believer, I know that if Jesus came back today and came across the homeless, He would do something radical to help them. So why would I not step out of my comfort zone to do something radical to help my brothers and sisters in need?

ONE

That Day

T HE FIRST TIME I CAME ACROSS A HOMELESS PERSON, I WAS
around the age of five. I remember that day like it was yesterday
because for one it was a gloomy day in San Diego, California. If you
know anything about San Diego, you will know that gloomy days are
rare. I was in the car with my nana, and we were on our way home
from church, which was located in the Logan Heights community
next to downtown.

I was so happy to be heading home from church. It seemed like
the pastor did not want to stop preaching that day. As a five-year-old,
even if Dr. Martin Luther King was preaching, it would have been
hard for me to sit there and listen. As we approached the nearest
stoplight to the church, I turned to my right of the four-corner
intersection and saw a man staring desperately into our car. There
was a shopping cart next to him filled with what appeared to be all
his belongings. Recycled soda cans and two-liter bottles filled one
of the boxes in the cart. There was also a makeshift bed and several
pants and shirts stretched across the cart.

I turned to my left and said, "Nana, why is he sitting there? I
think he needs help."

My nana looked at me, then at the man, and then up ahead, as
she tried to find the right thing to say to a curious five-year-old. She
continued to stare ahead at the light. It remained red. She turned
back to me, and settled on my wandering eyes. "Shel, that man don't
have a home. He's homeless. See, look at that sign next to him. You
see it?" Her voice became suddenly more direct.

I turned back toward the man hoping that he wouldn't notice
me staring. There was a sign that appeared to be made out of a
cardboard box. The words were written in black.

I quickly turned back to Nana to ask her what the sign said, but
before I could, she said, "Now let's stop staring at him. We have no
business staring at him."

"But what does that sign say, Nana?"

She didn't answer me. Instead, she drove forward as the light turned green. I could tell she wanted to answer my question, but now was not the time. Instead of going straight through the light, she made a quick right, adjacent to the corner where the homeless man was lying. Nana parked the car. Her focus shifted from me to the man.

As she opened the door, she said in a low voice, "Shel, stay in the car and lock your door."

Like most five-year-olds, I could not resist the questions oozing from my mind. "But, Nana, I want to go!"

Instead of responding or even acknowledging my demand, she slammed the door behind her. I started to feel the gravity of the moment. Nana telling me to lock the door indicated that our safety could be in jeopardy. My eyes did not lose sight of her as she walked across the front of the car to the sidewalk. I was more interested in what the man was going to do than anything else.

I watched the man as Nana cautiously walked toward him. As Nana inched closer, she reached into the pocket on the left side of her coat.

The man stood up simultaneously. He had some difficulty standing. As he stood fully erect, I realized he was much younger than he appeared when he was lying down. His aged appearance was likely due to wear and tear from living on the streets.

The two of them looked each other in the eyes. I could see Nana's lips moving and the young man nodding his head to every word that came out of her mouth. Nana handed him what appeared to be some money. The man kindly accepted what Nana gave him, and then he reached out and shook Nana's hand. He closed his eyes as he grasped her hand.

I felt something inside, but I couldn't comprehend what it was. My throat started to tighten, and a wave of emotion enveloped me. I shifted my attention back toward them. They appeared to be praying, and their heads were bowed. I couldn't help but feel something. My eyes were watering, and the knot in my throat tightened. I wiped the streaming tears with the back of my hand.

As I finished wiping my face, I looked over and saw Nana hugging the man. He seemed caught off guard by it. As Nana began to release, the man placed his arm around her with his head down. They both took a step back. The man still had his head down and appeared to be wiping tears from his eyes. My nana had just gone up to a complete stranger who was homeless and touched him in a way that was indescribable. She said her final goodbye and walked gracefully back to the car. I was curious about what had happened, but I said nothing the entire way home. Something had happened that could not be put into words, and that moment has always remained with me.

TWO

The Plan

THE DATE WAS JULY 11, 2018. IT WAS 5:50 A.M., AND I WAS driving my normal commute to the gym so I could get a workout in prior to work. The gym I work out in is next to what is called the homeless corridor. I have passed through the corridor almost daily for the past six years. And each day, it does not get easier. The hopelessness and the despair envelops the entire area, which makes it difficult to not feel something.

That morning, I did my normal routine—a forty-minute run on the treadmill and weights for an additional forty minutes—and then I called it quits and retreated to the locker room for my shower. As I was heading to the locker room, I noticed a middle-aged woman on one of the treadmills. I'd seen her camping out in the corridor on several occasions. She was walking gingerly, and her skin was leathery, likely from exposure to the sun. The path to the locker room was directly behind the line of treadmills.

As I neared the two treadmills in front of her, I could see she was walking gingerly because her shoes were barely holding together. I'd never seen such a worn-out pair of shoes. The shoe on her left foot no longer had a sole. Her left foot was essentially barefoot, and only the sides and the top of the shoe were intact. I was astonished that the shoe somehow remained on her foot. When I was a full treadmill past her, I felt an intense pull on my heart to do something. I ignored it and ended up not doing anything.

The entire day, I could not stop thinking about the woman at the gym. Moreover, I could not stop thinking about the fact that I did nothing. What was I supposed to do? The day was finally over, and I was relieved because I could not get her out of my thoughts. I drove into the driveway and eased into the garage.

My five-year-old son heard the garage door open and rushed out to greet me. "Hi, Daddy! You're finally home."

I quickly changed my energy and wiped away some of the sweat that was slowly dripping down both sides of my face. It was about 108 degrees on that July day, and it was probably an additional twenty degrees hotter inside the garage.

I grabbed my gym clothes and work stuff. "Hey, bud! Let's go inside so you can tell me all about your day!"

My one-year-old daughter made a quick dash toward me. "Dada! Dada!"

I thought she was going to embrace me, but she wanted me to chase her around the garage. The sweat was now running down my back. "Sweetie, let's go inside. It's hot in here!" I was hoping for a response but never received one. I added a little spice. "Sweetie, let's go inside. It's hot in here! If you don't come, Daddy is going to leave you here."

"No, Dada, no. Too hot."

I was anxious about the next day, because I desperately wanted to approach the lady. I propped myself on the couch and absorbed the emotional magnitude of the day. My wife, Nicole, emerged from upstairs. She knows me better than I know myself at times. She turned to me, sensing that something was amiss, and said, "Babe, why do you have that spacey look on your face? Did you have a bad day today or something? Vacation in two weeks—don't forget."

"Sweetie, my day was interesting. I saw this homeless woman working out, and I wanted to do something or say something, but I did neither. I've been struggling with this all day. I was asking myself, What would Nana have done—or even Jesus for that matter? Definitely not walk away." The smell of Nicole's chicken and potato dish was overtaking me, and before I could get comfortable on the couch, my focus shifted to dinner. I headed to the bathroom to wash my hands.

Nicole said, "Babe, don't get down on yourself. Just pray about it and go from there, but I am curious."

"Curious about what? Never mind that. I'm going to do something influential. That is at least my hope. I will see that woman again, and when I do, I will reach out to her." A thought crossed my mind. *I very possibly may not see the woman from the gym again, but as a man of faith, I trust that if it's meant for me to connect with her, I will.* That's at least what I told myself.

I could tell immediately that Nicole was not thrilled with me in that moment. I had sort of dismissed her question. She reluctantly turned toward me as I walked to the bathroom, and I could feel her energy piercing me in the back. She uttered, "Well, whatever you do, just pray about it first."

Jayden said, "Daddy, why are you being mean to Mommy?"

"I did not mean to be, bud. It just came out wrong. It will all be okay."

Nicole did not say much to me for the rest of the night, which put more stress on me. I was already feeling some internal pressure to come up with a plan, and now my own wife wasn't behind me because I had acted like a jerk.

I prayed that night, longer than usual, and I felt the magnitude of the plan. "Lord, please be with me as I formulate a plan to do something for the homeless. I know you are always in control, and I put all my faith in You. Amen."

My mind raced for the next two hours before I finally fell asleep. I kept thinking about what I was going to do. I had an idea. I rolled over and put the sheet over me. It was 2:24 a.m., and I could feel the air blowing on me from the vent above. I found a comfortable spot and finally closed my eyes.

I woke up the next morning. Friday had arrived, and I had an extra pep in my step because the weekend was within reach. I gathered my things and gently kissed Nicole and the sleeping kids.

Nicole turned to me and whispered, "I love you."

"Love you too, sweetie."

I felt much better as I headed to the gym. The morning was seemingly becoming brighter with each mile I drove. As I neared the gym, I passed a group of homeless individuals. Some appeared to be just waking up, and others remained sprawled out on the sidewalks. I came to a stop at the final light within the homeless encampment and noticed rows of bright flashing lights. When I looked closer, I saw five to seven police officers, along with several city officials, forcing people to wake up and pack up their belongings. A street sweeper was waiting. *This approach seemed to be abrupt and punitive. Where else can they go?*

The light turned green, and I focused my attention forward and tried to ignore the feeling coming over me. I felt hopeless. I wanted to do something. I wanted to help, but I did not know what that would entail.

Inside the gym, I cranked up the treadmill to a speed of 8.8. Five minutes into my run, I noticed my energy draining. My legs felt heavier with each stride. I kept looking around for the homeless woman, but she was nowhere to be found. I had one exercise left before it was time to head to the locker room. During the middle of my second set, I glanced to my left—and there she was. *She's here,* I thought. *She's here!* I stopped what I was doing and headed over to her.

I stepped on the treadmill immediately to her right, feeling extremely nervous, and said, "Hi, ma'am. How are you doing this morning?"

"I'm doing great," she replied.

"I am glad to hear. Quick question. Is it okay if I bless you with a new pair of shoes? I noticed—"

"You noticed what?"

"Um, I noticed—"

"I don't need no new shoes. There's nothing wrong with these shoes. Nothing!"

I was speechless. I had not expected that reaction. She appeared to be irritated by my inquiry, but she kept a smile on her face.

"Ma'am, I hope I did not offend you. I just thought I would ask."

"Thank you for asking, but I am okay. You go and have a nice day."

"Thank you, ma'am. Take care." I stepped off the treadmill not knowing how to feel. I was utterly confused. I knew she was a woman with a lot of pride, and I had to respect that.

I saw one of my friends in the locker room. Jason was in his sixties and knew a lot about everything. "Hey, Sheldon. How goes it?"

"It's going, Jason. I just had a weird exchange with a homeless woman on the treadmill."

"Weird exchange, huh? What happened, my friend? I certainly want to know. I am just in awe of how resourceful some of the homeless are, especially those who come to this gym. I think it's great that they purchase a membership to work out—and some of them just come in to do their hygiene."

"Yeah, Jason. I agree with you. I certainly have a lot of respect for them, but I am struggling with that homeless woman. Do you know the one I'm talking about?"

"Yes, I do."

"Well, I'm not sure if you ever looked down at her shoes, but they are worn to the core. I felt it on my heart to buy her a new pair of shoes, and I was simply going to ask her what her shoe size was, assuming, of course, if she said she could use a new pair."

"So, she told you no?"

"Basically, she said no, but it was more like a hell no—with a smile."

Jason sat down and put his head down. I could tell that what I shared had caused him to feel something. He lifted his head after about twenty seconds.

I sat down to meet him at eye level.

With tears streaming from his eyes, he said, "Look at what humanity has done. I just … I just can't anymore. I can't understand us and how we treat people."

I'd known Jason for close to seven years, and I'd never seen him react that way to anything. I headed to work with Jason and the woman from the gym on my mind. Their reactions threw me for a loop. More than ever, I felt called to finalize my plan.

When I finally arrived at work, my head was spinning from my interactions at the gym. During my lunch break, I decided to research ideas about my homeless project since the ideas I had formulated during the night no longer seemed feasible. My main idea was to partner with several community providers to do a massive resource drive. I wanted individuals experiencing homelessness to get plugged into services such as mental health and substance abuse counseling and medical care. As a licensed mental health professional, I was already wearing that hat, and I felt called to do something more profound.

I came across two courageous professional athletes who had immersed themselves for a day as undercover homeless men to raise awareness for homelessness. I thought the idea was brilliant! Wanting to tailor the idea to be more of my own, I decided that forty-eight hours out on the streets would be a better length of time for me. I would be alone with no money, water, or food. I would have to earn everything I would receive. I wanted to submerge myself in what it truly felt like to be homeless. I wanted to know what the lady from the gym felt and what numerous homeless clients I'd had over the years had experienced. I was really going to do this.

August 31, 2018, to September 2, 2018, would be the dates. Labor Day weekend would allow for extra time to recover because I was probably going to need it. I finally felt at peace, but then I remembered my wife. *How will she receive this? Will she support me putting myself out there? I have a family to support—and God forbid if something happened to me. It wasn't that long ago when the news reported a man walking around the Las Vegas area, randomly killing homeless people. In addition to the safety risks, there are the health risks. Hepatitis B, among other illnesses, was a big risk.*

Almost two weeks had gone by before I shared my idea with Nicole. We were in San Diego, California, for a family reunion, and on the final night of an amazing and beautiful trip, I decided to break the news to her. On vacation, she was in her most relaxed state. The kids were exhausted from the day's activities and fell asleep as soon as their heads hit the pillows. Nicole was on one of the beds, nursing Arianna to sleep, and Jayden slept peacefully beside me.

"Hey, sweetie. Is Arianna asleep," I whispered.

"Not quite yet, but she is getting there. Give her five more minutes," Nicole replied.

I waited a few long minutes before I spoke. "I have something I want to share with you. It's my plan for the homeless project."

"Go ahead and spit it out. I am curious to hear about it. Hopefully it's not nothing crazy." She chuckled.

I knew right then she was not going to completely support my plan. I knew her too well. "So, this is what it is. I am going undercover for two days as a homeless male—or roughly forty-eight hours."

"Wait, wait, wait! Going undercover as a homeless person?"

"Yep."

"Where are we talking? Downtown—or outside of our home?"

"Let me explain it. Just hear me out. That's all I am asking. Okay?"

"Sure, whatever, Sheldon."

"Are you mad at me, sweetie?"

"Not mad, just frustrated because it seems like you thought all this out without even considering me. But, whatever, go ahead."

"So, my plan is to live on the streets downtown, and you know, do it to raise awareness for homelessness. I want to really experience it, so I am going to go out there without any food, water, phone, or anything."

"Well, what if I want to check on you or what if something ... what if something bad happens to you? How would I know?

Nicole's response in that moment was a lot for me to take in, and I needed to validate her. I said, "I appreciate your concerns. They are all valid, you know, and um, I have thought about the risks to my well-being. Anything can happen out there, but my trust in God is greater than any fear or threat that may be present."

"Shel, I know your faith is strong, but that still does not subtract from my fear of something bad happening to you. Sometimes I think you forget you have a family."

"That's completely not fair!" I was getting irritated.

"Shh! You're getting loud."

"Sorry. This is something that is important to me. As someone who has been marginalized at different points of my life, I always wished I had someone to speak up for me— someone who other people would listen to. No matter how many times I shared my pain with others, it never mattered. I have a real opportunity here to lend a voice to the homeless so that more can be done to address the issue. I don't know what will come of it, but I don't want to look back with regret because I did not follow through with something that was important to me."

"I respect your passion and you wanting to help the homeless and all, but I don't want anything to happen to you. That's all."

"And you have to trust me that if I thought something bad was going to happen to me, I would not follow through with it. I have prayed about it, and I am at peace with it."

"So, you were going to do this no matter what I said?"

I could sense her disappointment and pain that I didn't consider her. "Kind of, but I want your blessing—along with your suggestions. I want you to be part of this."

THREE

The Big Day

F OR A MONTH OR SO, I DROVE BY THE AREAS I PLANNED ON frequenting just to have a sense of what to expect. I would drive by after work, sometimes during the middle of the day, and on the weekends when Las Vegas was really jumping. When I couldn't sleep one morning, I threw on some clothes and jumped into my car. Before leaving the house, I checked the time. It was 3:05 a.m.

Out on the streets, I was amazed by how calm everything seemed. Most of the individuals on the streets were sleeping. I only saw a handful of stragglers wandering aimlessly, with nowhere to go. As I headed west on Bonanza Avenue, I hooked a left on North City Parkway and drove for a quarter mile before coming to an intersection. As I waited for the light to turn green, I had a moment to reflect on a location where I could sleep at night. Slightly to my right, about eighty feet across from me, was a green power box. It was positioned in the desert sand, just beyond the sidewalk that connected to a bus stop. The area evoked a calmness in me. The darkness was backlit by the flashing lights from the Strip. It was breathtaking, but it was also "safe."

The light finally turned green, but instead of turning left, I drove straight through the intersection and parked on the side of the street. As I got out of my car, I noticed two homeless men across the street. One appeared to be sleeping, and the other man was looking directly at me. I'm sure he was wondering what I was doing, but I paid him no mind.

I inched closer to what likely would serve as my weekend home, and I examined the power box closely. There was a bus stop a few feet away and the light from the bus stop provided an element of safety. If something happened to me, I would not be completely isolated. Before driving off, I sat on top of the power box and watched the downtown Las Vegas lights dancing in rapid succession. The concrete slab would be perfect for stretching my legs. I jumped back in my car, I was ready to sleep. I had an hour before it was time to wake up and start my day.

August 31 was finally here. Nicole and I had discussed how keeping my daily routine the same—waking up at five, working out at the gym, going to work for a full day, and going home to eat dinner as a family—would benefit my mental state. I needed to distract myself as much as possible to keep my anxiety at a manageable level.

I slept surprisingly well considering everything that was at stake. I typically prayed at night, and I occasionally prayed in the morning after I woke up, but I felt it was pertinent to thank my heavenly Father for today—and for the position He put me in to help others. "Dear God, I come to you in the name of Jesus. I thank you for this day and every day You bless us with. I'm so grateful for putting on my heart the journey I am about to experience to help others in need. Please, Lord, I just ask that you not only watch over my well-being while I am out there, but the well-being of the rest of Your people who are out there struggling. Amen."

A sense of peace and calm came over me in that moment. I felt invincible—at least for the time being.

I exited the freeway and headed to the gym for the last time before I hit the streets. It was already eighty-eight degrees, and the high for the day would be 105. Those temperatures would remain for the weekend, which would make things even more challenging for me. I felt the anxiety setting in, and I quickly shifted my focus.

The gym was quieter than normal. When I entered, Evelyn, the gym clerk at the front desk, greeted me with a smile. "Good morning, Sheldon! Happy Friday to you!"

"Good morning, and happy Friday to you as well, Evelyn. I can't get over how fast the week has gone. Summer will be over in a blink of an eye."

"Yes, it will! Well, have a good workout."

"Thank you!" I exclaimed as I headed for the treadmill.

Looking around the gym as I worked out, I hoped to see the homeless lady who had inspired me beyond words. I wanted to tell her about my idea and how she had lit a fire under me—one that I never saw coming. I wanted to tell her those things and hear her story. Unfortunately, that would have to wait since she is nowhere to be found. I finished my last workout and headed to the showers. I found myself alone in the locker room, a rare event. In the shower, in a moment of solace, I finally started to truly embrace what I was about to do. I still had a grinding nine-hour workday to get through, but I started to gain a sense of what was ahead of me.

As I headed out the gym door, I said, "Have a good rest of the day, Evelyn, and try not to work too hard!"

"Thank you, Sheldon, and the same to you."

"I likely won't be here much of the following week." I felt the need to share. "I will be recovering from a weekend adventure!"

Evelyn leaned forward and said, "Really, where are you going?"

"I can't really tell you now, but I promise to tell you when I come back."

I felt like I had let Evelyn down, and I could tell she was disappointed because I usually told her about my weekend happenings. Feeling bad about the whole thing, I said, "You will be the first to know when it's all over."

"I'm going to hold you to that," she said with a smile.

Each day, after arriving at work, I gave Nicole a call to let her know that I made it in okay. "Hello. Good morning, sweetie."

"Morning, babe, how goes it?"

"It's going."

"Are you ready for tonight? It's almost that time."

"Yeah, I know. It's just been a weird day so far. You know me. I read into stuff probably too much. The day just has not gone as I expected."

"What do you mean? Don't tell me you are having second thoughts?" Nicole seemed somewhat excited about the prospect of me not following through with the forty-eight-hour project. *I can't quite blame her. I know she's going to be worried to death about me. I also know it took a lot for her to get behind me on this, and I'm sure a part of her would be disappointed if I backed out. That isn't an option I am even considering.* "Heck no! I'm in it. It's full steam ahead. The day has just been weird. The folks I normally see at the gym were not at the gym. Then I had this weird feeling when I was leaving."

"What happened? Did you see that homeless lady?"

"No, I did not see her, and nothing happened. It was just the front desk lady at the gym. Normally I talk to her about the weekend, and this time, I had to stop myself and not share what I was doing because I did not want her or anyone else to know."

"Oh, I see. Well, it will be fine. Just remember to pray throughout the day. I have to go, but I will talk to you later. Have a good day at work."

"Okay, thank you. I love you." I did not know how to read her. I sensed that she was still disappointed that I was continuing with the homeless endeavor.

"Love you too. Bye."

"Bye, sweetie," I said, wishing I had more time.

My workday went by extremely fast. I spent a lot of my downtime thinking about the weekend and trying to anticipate how it would go. I did not have a clue what was truly in store, which added to my anxiety. I looked at the clock and it was five minutes until five o'clock. My workday was almost over. I quickly gathered my belongings, went to the restroom, and left the building. Walking to my car, I could feel the magnitude of the moment slowly overwhelming me.

"Hey, Doc, have a good weekend!" a colleague yelled from across the parking lot. If only he knew what I was about to do.

"Thanks, you too!" I yelled back in an attempt to match his voice.

As I neared my car, one of our security guards was on patrol. He would be the last person I interacted with before heading home. "What's up, Doc?" he said with a concerned look. "You seem to have some stuff on your mind."

"Nothing, man, just ready to get home so I can get a head start on this weekend."

"It looked like you were in your head. You know, your thoughts."

"Wow, I didn't even think it was that obvious. But, yeah, I am hoping to do something to change the world this weekend, so that's what I was thinking subconsciously I guess." A smirk was beaming from my face. There was some truth to what I was saying, but it was a touch outlandish. My hope was that he would just let me go.

"Shit, change the world? You gots to put me on to that," he replied.

His inquisitiveness caught me off guard, but I managed to say, "Well, if you are as serious as you say you are, I will take you with me sometime. Let me see how this weekend goes, and then I will let you know."

"Doc, what is you doing, man?" He seemed to be getting irritated with me.

"Man, I'm just messing with you. I'm just going to head home and spend time with the family—that's all. Have a good weekend."

He seemed relieved. "Doc, don't do that again. I thought you was going to do some Martin Luther King stuff, man."

I couldn't do anything but smile. On my fifteen-minute drive to the house, I was feeling extremely anxious. I was a few hours away from being homeless, and I still didn't know what emotional state Nicole would be in. A part of me felt that even though she was supporting me, she still resented what I was doing because of all the risks involved. I mean, there was a legitimate possibility that something terrible could happen to me.

After I pulled into the driveway, I left the car running for a few minutes. Even at 5:22, it was a scalding 104 degrees, and turning off the car wouldn't be in my best interests. After looking around my neighborhood, I stared at my house. *What if this is the last time I am able to sit here and reflect like this? What if I never make it home? What if something bad happens to me?* I was making myself crazy. I spent a lot of time telling my clients to take control of their negative thoughts, and I probably should have taken a page out of my own book. Quickly replacing those negative thoughts, I thought, *I will be home in forty-eight hours. Nothing bad is going to happen to me. I am going to be able to help others.*

After several minutes, I rushed into the house. I was on a schedule. My pastors and fellow church members were meeting me at the park, our designated meeting place, at seven o'clock to pray over me before I headed out on my forty-eight hours. I still had to eat dinner, get changed, and most importantly, get myself mentally prepared.

"Daddy, Daddy, Daddy! You're home!" Jayden yelled as soon as I walked into the living room. He gave me this suffocating hug. He did not know what was going on. Nicole and I just told him that I was going to visit some friends for the weekend. Even though he was five years old, he was going on twenty-five in some respects.

"Hi, Jayden!"

My soon-to-be two-year-old, Arianna, and Nicole emerged from upstairs.

"Dada!" Arianna shouted when she spotted me. She immediately stretched her arms out, wanting me to hold her.

Nicole handed her off to me and kissed me hello. "How was your day?" Nicole asked as she started setting the table for dinner.

"Um, it was good, but—"

"Do you feel ready?"

"I'm as ready as I think I will be. I feel at peace, and I trust that God will watch over me while I'm out there." Arianna was trying to stick a piece of a Lego in my nose, but I gently pushed her hand away.

"I am starting to feel more nervous. After seeing you and the kids, it adds to the magnitude to this whole experience, you know?"

Arianna started to get restless in my arms. I think my body heat was increasing and becoming unbearable for her. I bent over so she could get down. She ran over to the couch and started playing with some of her toys.

As Nicole finished putting food on the plates, she whispered, "Please don't let anything happen to you—and be safe out there. That's my only ask."

"That's a big ask. I don't have complete control of what can happen to me out there—and I know you know that—but I have faith and peace that I will be protected. Just know that I would not have gone forward with this if I had any doubts."

Nicole walked over, and we embraced. I began to feel increasingly anxious. My heart was beating slightly faster, I felt warmer, and sweat was running down my back. The smell of dinner was making me feel a little nauseous.

"Don't worry, sweetie. It's all going to be okay, and I will be back before you know it. I need a second to wash my hands. I will be back." As I headed to the bathroom, I almost forgot to remind Nicole that my oldest brother would be coming in from Los Angeles and would be staying at the house while visiting a friend. "Oh, and Darryl will be here."

"I don't care about Darryl! Sorry, that came out wrong. You know what I mean."

"Well, he's the only other person that knows about the forty-eight hours besides you and our church family. He will be here for support and can help you with the kids."

"You are right. You are right. It will be nice to have some family around, I guess."

I washed my hands and splashed some cold water on my face. I immediately felt cooler and more relaxed. I bent over the sink and closed my eyes for a few seconds. My appetite started to return, and I felt a little more relaxed. I hurried to the dinner table where the rest of the family waited for me. I peeked at my watch; it was 5:47. Dinner was finally served. It was one of my favorite dishes: salmon, baked potatoes, and steamed vegetables. It was a simple meal, but it was a very important one since I did not know how much food I would consume over the next two days. We connected as a family as I said grace.

I couldn't even finish my dinner, which was strange because not having an appetite was never an issue for me.

"What's wrong?" Nicole asked.

"I'm full. I am full of nerves right now."

"Well, you better pile it on!"

"I will be good, sweetie. I need to go change. It's already almost six thirty and we have to be at the park at seven."

I went upstairs and put on the pair of shoes, pants, and a shirt that I purchased at a rescue mission the weekend before for less than ten dollars. Nicole's idea to take this experience to another level required that I did not have the resources or means to buy what I needed. Ten dollars was my budget.

As I was changing into my clothes for the first time, I realized how tight the pants were. *Oh well. There's nothing I can do about it now.* I put my shirt on and looked at myself in the mirror for the final time. My beard, which I'd been growing out for the past three months, looked patchy and out of sorts, perfect for my objective. The hair on the top of my head was also quite long. As I examined myself from head to toe, I almost didn't recognize myself. My thoughts raced again. *What is it going to be like out there? How will I be treated by others? Is something bad going to happen to me?* I ran downstairs and threw on the shoes. We had to be at the park in eight minutes.

"Let's go, guys! Let's go!" I rushed everyone to the car. "Does everyone have everything?"

"Babe, your mini tote bag is over there next to the door."

"Thanks!" The tote bag was more of a tote bag than tote bag, and it held my journal, two bottles of water, a piece of cardboard to make a sign, and a pen.

"Sweetie, I only need one bottle of water."

"No, please take the two—just in case. It's going to be very hot this weekend."

"You are right."

Nicole yelled out of the car window, "Do you have your driver's license?"

"Shoot. I left it upstairs!" I ran back into the house, found it on the dresser, and stuck it in my sock.

As we headed outside of our neighborhood, I could see flashing lights illuminating the dark sky. I could tell the lights were coming from the main street adjacent to our neighborhood. The street is partially blocked, and I can't turn left to head to the freeway. There appeared to be a bad car accident.

"Dang it! Now we are going to be late. Shoot! Nicole, can you please text one of the pastors to let them know that we are running late?"

We finally arrive at the park after several detours at 7:18. The hint of light that was visible when we left the house was gone, which mattered because we were meeting at a park within the homeless corridor that bordered a neighborhood of abandoned housing projects. The area was notorious for drug deals, prostitution, and violence—not the best place to be after dark. I was more concerned with some of my church members. Many of them had likely never experienced that type of environment.

I parked our SUV behind the row of cars belonging to our church members. I could see them excitedly awaiting our arrival. I stepped out first and helped Nicole get Jayden and Arianna out of their car seats. Before Nicole picked up Arianna, she handed me my tote bag. I double-checked to make sure everything was in there.

"Thank you," I whispered. My voice felt slightly paralyzed from the anxiety I was starting to feel again.

"You are welcome. You ready?"

"Yep!"

"Daddy, there's lots of people here. Are they here for you?" Jayden asked.

"Yes, they are from church and will be praying over us." I grabbed his hand, and we walked toward the eight or so church members. I greeted everyone individually.

"Thank you so much for being here. Words can't describe how appreciative I am," I said to each church member, including our three pastors.

Our senior pastor approached me and said, "Good evening, Doc. We are glad you, Nicole, and the kids are here. I commend you for doing what you are to shed light on such an important topic in addition to your willingness to help those in need."

"Thank you, Pastor," I responded in a soft voice. I feel Nicole inching closer to my side. I put my left hand around her and held Jayden's hand with my right hand.

"Would anyone like to pray for our faithful servant, Sheldon, during this time?" the pastor asked.

"Sure, I would like to go," Linda said. She was one of our close friends in the church. "Lord, God, I thank you for your good and faithful servant Sheldon as he is not turning a cold shoulder to this really important issue that affects our city. He is willing, on Your command, to just walk right into the depths."

Several others took turns praying. I could see Nicole wiping away her tears. I was tearing up more and more with each prayer. Our senior pastor closed us out in prayer.

This is it. It is time to finally say goodbye to everyone, including my family. My anxiety disappeared, and I felt an imaginary armor come over me. I thanked everyone again for coming out and gave my final embraces. It was much harder to say goodbye to Nicole and the kids than I thought it would be.

A spiritual send-off with fellow church members

"Babe, this is it. God has you now. Just be careful out there," Nicole said as she wiped away more tears.

"I will, sweetie. I promise. This isn't about me—it's for all the people struggling out here." I bent down and said goodbye to Jayden. "Bud, I love you. Be good for Mommy and be a big, big brother to Arianna. I will be back in a couple of days."

"Bye, Dad. Have fun camping," he said.

I can't even remember if that's where we told him I was going for the weekend. I reached over and kissed Arianna. "Bye, Mamas." She seemed like she was still trying to process what was happening.

Everyone left, and the park was empty. I waited for Nicole to drive off safely, and I waved as she drove past me into the desert night.

This is it.

FOUR

The First Eight

I NO LONGER HAD IMMEDIATE ACCESS TO THE TIME. THERE WAS a large clock on top of one of the downtown hotels, but I was not close enough to see it. I assumed it was around eight o'clock. As I walked away from the park, I wanted to stop by the Fremont Street Experience in downtown. Although it was less than a mile away, I realized right away that the streets appeared to be much darker walking than when driving. Every three or four steps, I quickly looked behind me just to make sure nobody was following me.

The sidewalk abruptly ended right beneath my feet, and I stopped to see what was going on. As I measured the street and my surroundings, I noticed that the street had narrowed. I drove up and down that street at least ten times a week, but I never knew that stretch of winding road did not contain a sidewalk. The other side of the street did have a sidewalk, but it was occupied with people camping out.

I remained on the side of the street without the sidewalk, and several people walked past me.

"Hey, man, you gots some spare change or spare cigs?" a man asked.

"No sorry. I have neither one," I said.

The man kept walking. I found it prudent to do the same thing as cars were whisking by at high speed, and I was literally walking down a dimly lit street. My stride started to pick up. I don't want to get hit by a car from behind. A stretch of sidewalk emerged, and I crossed the street. I looked to my left and saw rows of homeless people camped out along the sidewalk. Some were spilling into the street, and directly behind them was one of the town's rescue missions.

I felt an urge to urinate. The glass of Powerade I had downed before I left the house was starting to kick in. The gym I frequented was about a hundred feet ahead, which was perfect timing. With each step I took, the urge became a little more pronounced. The only way to the main entrance of the gym was to enter through the attached parking garage. Several other businesses and a government building shared the same garage. Because of the high crime in the area, security guards patrolled the building around the clock.

Six steps after I entered the parking garage, someone yelled, "Hey, you can't be in here!"

I turned around to track the voice, but I didn't see anyone. I realized security was trying to get my attention via an intercom that was connected to the toll at the entrance of the parking garage. I walked over to the intercom and said, "Hello, sir, I am just going to enter the gym to use the restroom."

"I am afraid you can't do that. You must leave these premises immediately—or you will be considered trespassing!"

I was starting to get frustrated—and I urgently had to use the restroom. Instead of walking away and finding a nearby bush or wall, I said, "Look, sir, I am actually a member of this gym—and I have the right to enter to use the restroom if I want to. I work out at this gym almost every day." I started walking as fast as I could, considering the full bladder that was slowing me down.

As I neared the entrance, two security guards started walking toward me. "Please stop right there!"

"Listen, I am a member of this gym, and I have to use the restroom."

They didn't say anything, and I proceeded to the double doors at the gym entrance. They followed right behind, almost in sync with my every step.

Wow, is this how you treat people?

"Good evening," the lady at the front desk said.

"Good evening. I hope yours is better than mine. Look, these security guards are harassing me. I'm a member of this gym, and I just need to use the restroom."

One of the security guards said, "Susan, can you please verify that this man is a member?"

The gym used a fingerprint check-in system, and I went ahead and checked in.

Susan had me verify my date of birth and address and said, "He's good to go, guys."

Since I always went in the mornings, I never saw the evening gym staff or security guards. One of the security guards said, "Sheldon, what are you doing walking around like this? You look real suspicious, man."

I was feeling defiant. "Walking around like what? I mean, you guys should be mindful of how you speak to people. I felt really—"

"We apologize for the mix-up. We just thought you were, you know, we get lots of homeless folk down here, you know, and we thought you were one of them."

I knew the security officers were just doing their jobs, but I wanted them to understand that I was a human being—and they needed to utilize more sensitivity.

"Just be mindful of how you talk to people. They, the people who are homeless, are people too and have feelings just like all four of us." How would this situation have unfolded if I did not recognize one of them? I could not help but think of the scores of homeless who passed through that building each day. I felt for them.

When I finished using the restroom, I didn't know what to think. I felt good about relieving my bladder, but I was frustrated by the way I had been treated. As I exited the building, I headed toward downtown Las Vegas. Each step I took, the brighter the sky became above me. I walked through the four-lane tunnel, and I almost stepped on a man who was in a deep sleep in the middle of the sidewalk. My attention completely shifted. I did not want to stop and stare, but the man did not even appear to be alive. Reality started to hit me. For the time being, I was no longer a privileged man who could ignore the profound issue of homelessness. I couldn't simply jump in my car and drive to my four-bedroom house and pretend that the problem I was staring at right in front of me did not exist.

I maneuvered around the man, wondering how someone could comfortably sleep on a public sidewalk with people passing by—not to mention the rock-hard concrete. *That is his reality,* I thought, *and soon it will be mine.* I continued to walk toward the bright flashing lights. The incline of the tunnel increased for the next seventy feet or so. There was some lighting in the tunnel, but it was not enough to make me feel comfortable. The smell of urine and rotten food permeated my senses. Two mice ran directly in front of me from the other side of the street, which caused me to stop in my tracks. When I felt comfortable again, I put one foot in front of the other and headed out of the tunnel. When I reached an area where the sidewalk began to level off, I could feel the sweat streaming down my back and chest. Walking up the tunnel was a nice little workout.

On the corner, I looked behind me and saw a group of three middle-aged men. They were sitting on top of sleeping bags and asking for money. I noticed that one of the men did not have any legs.

One of the men made eye contact with me and said, "Yo, son, do you have at least a few dollars?"

"I'm so sorry, sir, but I don't have any money myself. I'm trying to look for a few too." I felt compelled to give, but I realized that I did not have anything to give them. I reached in my tote bag and pulled out one of my bottles of water. "Would this work? It's not money, but—"

"Yo, thank you man," the man without legs said as he reached out his arms.

"It's the least I could do. You guys, take care and be safe out here," I said.

"Thank you," all three of them said in unison.

The light turned green, and I briskly walked along the crosswalk.

I looked at the three men, and they were taking turns drinking out of the water bottle. By the time I made it across the street, the water was gone. *How did they end up in their predicament? What happened to that man's legs?* So many questions left unanswered, but it would likely become more apparent as the weekend passed.

As I neared my destination for the night, several tourists walked past me. They did not make eye contact with me. I didn't think too much of it. I crossed one more street, illegally, and the foot traffic increased. I heard live music in the background and followed a crowd down a narrow path to the Fremont Street Experience.

"Hey, you got a smoke?" a young girl asked me.

"Naw, I don't smoke. Sorry," I said.

She was with a group of six or seven teenagers. Their clothes were worn and tattered, and I looked down at their shoes to further assess their situation. Most teenagers took pride in their shoe selection, a symbol of self-actualization, but the plight of this group of teenagers was different. One of the boys had a hole on the side of his shoe, showing his bare feet, and one of the girls had on two mismatched, tattered shoes.

"You smoke bud? We are trying to get lit, homie."

"Naw, I don't do that either. What are you guys doing out here? You all look young." I could not help myself. I had to ask.

"That's an, um, that's a difficult one," one of the boys responded.

"Joe, let's go. There's Brit and Amy!" another one of the teens yelled. They all took off toward a crowd of people gathered around a street performer.

"Later, dude!" one from the bunch yelled.

I wanted to do something or at least say something. The bulk of my clinical and professional experience had been working with adolescents. They could be difficult to reach at times, but I felt like I possessed a unique ability to connect with them. I had an opportunity to connect and hear their stories, but I had let the opportunity slip away. If only I could offer them some words of encouragement. "Damn it!" I repeated to myself several times.

After a few more steps, the narrow path finally connected to the Fremont Street Experience. The loud noise and the loads of people immediately jumped out at me. I noticed a long stretch of wall to my immediate left. It appeared to be some type of advertisement. I quickly walked over to the wall to minimize the overwhelming feeling I was having. I placed my feet slightly in front of me so that my butt was completely supported by the wall. I hadn't looked at the time for what appeared to be an eternity.

A tall White man in a suit slowly walked past me.

"Excuse me, sir. Can you please tell me the time?"

The man looked down at his watch, barely looking up to acknowledge me. "It's five after nine."

Before I could say thank you, he disappeared into the crowd. I was starting to wonder if people could tell I was homeless. Some of my interactions, or lack thereof, were innocuous—but also bizarre. It seemed like those who were homeless were the only ones who interacted with me. No, maybe it was just in my head.

Standing about a football field away from me was a large stage. A live band just finished playing a set. As the noise level decreased, it was replaced by loud music blaring from overhead speakers. Immediately in front of me were several groups of street performers. Two women and two men were playing the parts of the Joker, Edward Scissorhands, Cinderella, and Minnie Mouse. Their face paint looked very professional. To the right of them, a guy in his thirties was doing magic tricks and drawing a large crowd. The live music and entertainment provided enough distraction to make me forget my invisibility.

I watched the crowd for another ten minutes and noticed a few stares, but I didn't think anything of it. All of a sudden, a Hispanic family stood directly in front of me. The two middle-aged parents and three teenagers, two girls and a boy, were probably arm's length away.

"Let's go to the Golden Nugget. The sharks are there," one of them said.

I remembered taking my son there the previous year. He was fascinated by sharks, and watching the joy on his face as the sharks swam directly in front of him was priceless. That was a fun bonding experience. Now, as I stood here, I wondered if I would even be allowed inside. *How quickly your reality can change.*

The side entrance to the Golden Nugget Hotel and Casino was diagonally across from where I was sitting. One of the girls turned toward me and stared. I stared back and noticed that she looked very familiar. *Where do I know her from?* She looked back at me a second time before walking away with her family.

It hit me! *She is one of my former college students! Wow, she did not even recognize me. Or did she?* I told myself that she just did not recognize me, which was a much easier reality to digest. I'd taught hundreds of students over the years, but she had always stood out because of her desire to learn. She often stayed after class to ask questions or made appointments to talk during my office hours. I always appreciated her tenacity. I didn't know how I would have handled the situation if she recognized me and still chose to walk away.

After standing for a good thirty minutes, my legs began feeling fatigued. Instead of sitting down, I decided to head down in the opposite direction of the stage to see what else was going on. The farther I walked, the more crowded it became. The strong smells of cigarettes, marijuana, and perfume began to irritate my eyes and make them water. I saw nearly naked women, dressed as nuns, walking around with signs and several showgirls who left nothing to the imagination.

After walking around aimlessly for another fifteen minutes, I decided to head back to my spot. As I got closer, I saw a man smoking a cigarette. Feeling a bit territorial, I wanted to question why he was sitting there, but at the same time, I thought I could use the company.

"Hey man, what's up," the man asked. "You want to smoke some weed? I also gots some beer."

"Nothing much. Just needing a resting spot, and I am good. Thank you," I said.

"I feel you, bro. I been grinding on these shitty streets all damn day! There are some big college football games on tomorrow. I gots to win big, my man. You know what I'm sayin', right? You play at all?

"Play?" I did not know what he meant.

"Bro, is you slow? Sports betting! You know. You gamble, man?" He chuckled.

"Oh, my bad. I didn't know what you were saying. No, I don't gamble, and I'm not slow. I do like sports, especially college football. I did not quite understand what you were getting at. What's your name?"

"My name is Michael. The ladies calls me, um, Big Mike, you know, but you can call me Michael."

"Yeah I don't want to be calling you Big Mike then. My name is Sheldon." I reached out to shake Michael's hand.

Michael turned to me with a serious look on his face. "You out here hustling, man? It's slim pickings, you know? Gotta hit this ticket big! You want some of these seeds, man, or a smoke?"

"Naw, Michael. I'm just out here chilling right now. I usually stay at one of the nearby shelters, but they were all full, so I'm just posted tonight. Also, I don't smoke, but thanks for asking. And the sunflower seeds? I am good—thanks." I felt kind of bad lying about my actual predicament, but I had to come up with something.

"Is it cool if I, um, if I calls you Shel?"

"Sure. Most of my friends and family call me that. All good."

"Cool then, Shel. Well check this out. I want you to give me some of your thoughts on some of these college games tomorrow, you know? I gots to win at least two hundred bucks so I can stay at the Siegel Suites through the weekend. You feel me?"

"No doubt, Michael." I was being more mindful of my vernacular. I could talk a little street slang if I needed to. I noticed Michael was getting comfortable with me, and I was starting to get comfortable with him.

"Let me see the ticket, Michael."

He handed me all the games with the spreads. I didn't know all the ins and outs of the spreads and the lines, but I did know what teams to pick to give him the best possible chance to win. I loved college football and had a good feel for a lot of the teams. So, are you from Vegas—or are you from elsewhere like mostly everyone else?"

Michael laughed and said, "I am from Miami. Been in Vegas for like three or four years, you know? I lost everything in Miami and decided to come here to chase the American dream, you know, man. Shit's crazy, man. I lost everything back there. My wife, my son, my—"

A seminude woman walked toward us and said, "Hey, guys. Do you want to have some fun tonight?"

I quickly said, "No, I am good, but thanks for asking."

Michael jumped up and walked over to the lady. Without saying a word, the two of them disappeared. What remained of Michael was his tote bag, cup of beer, a full pack of cigarettes, and sunflower seeds. I scooted down a little farther in case there was anything illegal in his tote bag. The last thing I needed was to get arrested and placed in jail for someone else's stuff. I took in my surroundings and wondered when Michael was going to resurface. I didn't know what to feel. The anxiety from earlier had subsided, and I was starting to feel a bit hungry. My thoughts shifted to where I was going to get money and what I was going to eat.

It had been about thirty minutes since I had seen Michael, and I remained in my same spot, sitting up against the wall. The only time I moved was when I needed to stretch my legs, which was probably more of a reprieve for my bottom from the hard concrete.

The band was about to play the second song of their set, and the lead guitarist shouted, "Las Vegas, are you having a great time?"

The crowd roared back in approval. As I looked around, I could tell right away that he was not addressing everyone in the venue. I saw a number of folks, like Michael, experiencing some form of despair.

As the night progressed, I saw more homeless men and women and even a few teenagers who, like me, did not know where their next meal would come from. I started to feel more connected to my current reality and less connected to the everyday world I thought I knew.

There was still no sign of Michael. I continued to keep an eye on his belongings since it seemed to be the right thing to do. I glanced directly in front of me, and the magic guy was still performing tricks. *He must be making a killing on tips since there is a consistent crowd in front of him.* I started to think about tomorrow morning and the rest of the weekend. *What am I going to eat? Where am I going to get money from? Where am I going to sleep?* The thoughts flooding my head were triggered by my sudden hunger and tiredness. I took a few sips of my water, wanting to preserve what I could.

Three young male tourists walked toward me. One appeared to be Hispanic, and the other two appeared to be Asian. All of them were holding beers.

"Hey, take a picture of me in front of that wall," one of them said.

One of the Asian men was designated as the photographer.

I thought they would just keep walking past me like the hundreds of other tourists, but the Hispanic man started walking toward me. He appeared to want to have his picture taken in front of the wall I was sitting against.

I scooted closer to Michael's belongings to avoid being in the picture. As they moved closer, I could see that all three men appeared to be in their twenties.

The Hispanic man stopped, turned, and posed as the camera flashed. "One more bro, one more!" The camera flashed one last time, and he walked over to his friends. They congregated for forty seconds or so and then walked to a souvenir shop.

The Hispanic man headed in my direction, and a wave of anxiety overcame me. *What does this man want from me?*

He stopped, bent over, and said, "Hey, how are you doing?"

"I am doing okay. Just chilling." I still did not know what to expect.

"That's cool. Are you homeless by any chance?"

Wow, what a great way to start a conversation. That took a lot of guts. "Yes, I am homeless, man. Like for the past two years, on and off, you know?" It was weird to say it out loud and identify myself as not having anywhere to go and no place to call home.

"Sorry, I did not mean to come off like that. You know, insensitive and whatnot. Me and my friends saw you sitting over here, and I told them that I wanted to talk to you because you seemed, um, alone. Is it okay if I sit down here with you?"

"Man, I appreciate you coming over. Sure, have a seat," I said. *It is nice to cross opposite worlds with someone—even if it is for a short period of time.* "So, what is your name?"

"Danny, but you can call me Dan. That's what most of my friends call me." He adjusted his legs, trying to find a comfortable position. "So, what's your name?"

"Sheldon."

"That's a pretty unique name. Where are you from, Sheldon?"

"I am originally from San Diego, but I have lived here in Vegas for the past eight years. Where are you from?"

He gulped some of his beer. "I'm from the Bay Area. Me and my two friends are in the Navy, and we, um, we are currently stationed in San Diego. You are from there!"

"Yep, that's home for me."

"So, how did you end up out here in the City of Sin, of all places?"

"To be honest, it's an extremely long, long, long story." I did not know what else to say, so I figured that would get him to change the subject.

"Sheldon, I love San Diego, and that's coming from a Bay Area native. Your city is very beautiful, but this homeless thing—my heart just breaks for you and the many others. Sometimes I wish I could do more to help solve homelessness, but I know it's a very complex issue with many layers."

"That is the unfortunate reality. It's very hard, especially to see people suffering." I could feel the weight of the topic.

"Sheldon, you can get through this. Man, I don't know your situation, but I know you will get back on your feet real soon."

"I appreciate that, Dan."

When Dan's friends reappeared from the souvenir shop, he glanced at them and held up a finger. He refocused his thoughts and attention on me. "I will be praying for you. Stay strong, stay strong." He stood up and held out his beer. "Hey, do you want this?"

"No, thanks. I don't drink."

He reached in his back pocket and pulled out his wallet. "Please, Sheldon, at least take this money." He handed me a twenty-dollar bill.

I felt a visceral reaction of pure joy. I could eat! I'd never felt so happy to touch a twenty-dollar bill. "Thank you so much." I hurriedly placed the money in my pocket, hoping he wouldn't change his mind.

Dan took two steps toward his friends, and then he turned back to me. "You've got this. You will get through this. God bless you."

The three of them disappeared into the crowd.

I was feeling a mix of emotions. To come across someone so

generous and caring meant a lot. He took the time to sit down and chat with me when he could have been doing what every other tourist was doing. I felt so encouraged knowing there were truly good people in this world. *Why me? I'm sure I am not the only homeless person he came across, but I am likely the only one he spent time with. So why? I'm not better or different than anyone else.*

Michael reappeared about five minutes after Dan took off with his buddies.

"Hey, man. I'm back. I had to take care of some business, you know? That ho, you know, is the sister of this pimp I owe money to. I had her lead me to him so I could pay him part of what I owe. I got to pay him the rest of the money by tomorrow, so shit, I gots to win some of these games tomorrow, you know, you know what I sayin', man?"

"What happens if you come up short, you know? What will happen?"

"Shit, I just get dealt wit, you know? I just get dealt wit. It is what it is. I gots no worries, man."

"Damn, Mike, I mean Michael, that is real. So, you just going to deal with the consequences if you don't win tomorrow?"

"I gots no fucking choice, man!" Michael appeared to be getting aggravated by my questions.

I felt the need to apologize to him and the predicament he was in. I couldn't help but think of all those people living like Michael. "Sorry. I didn't mean to upset you. I just don't want anything bad to happen, you know? I will be praying for you tonight for sure." I remained in my spot.

Michael said, "I'm abouts to get some more beer. You wants some?"

"Naw. I'm good, but thanks."

Michael hurried off again, leaving me alone with my thoughts. I kind of missed his presence. *He is an interesting fellow, full of energy and humor—a nice distraction to say the least—but I wonder why he keeps buying beers despite what lies ahead for him. Shouldn't he be saving every penny?* A part of me wanted to give him the twenty dollars I was just blessed with. *What would he do with it? Would he drink or smoke it all up?* The uncertainty of not having money or even knowing when that next buck would come was not something I was ready to experience so soon.

About twenty minutes passed since Michael's departure. I continued to watch the hustle and bustle of people walking past me, the street performers in front of me, the band playing on the stage to my right, loud music blasting to my left, and the folks zip-lining up above me. Despite all the excitement surrounding me, I still felt invisible. I wondered if the thousands of folks who kept passing by even knew that I was sitting here—or did they know and make a conscious choice to not acknowledge someone who was not like them. In reality, I *was* them. Their actions certainly did not indicate that. I just wanted someone to smile at me, make eye contact, or say a simple hello. *Are those things so hard to ask for? Well, maybe they are when you are invisible.*

I sipped the last of my water. Just like that, all my fluids were gone. I noticed the crowd in front of me was starting to thin out. It had to be around midnight, but I was not quite sure. I turned toward the stage and saw people dancing, hugging, socializing, and simply having a good time. The glitz and glam of the casino's bright lights pulsated in the background.

I also saw the depressed looks on the faces on the homeless folks who were likely camping nearby, doing what they could to survive. It was an interesting dichotomy because there was so much darkness and despair surrounding me. It was as if the glamour was a deliberate attempt to mask the realities of the world that nobody wanted to speak of.

My despair deepened when I saw what appeared to be a homeless veteran pass by in an electric wheelchair. Both of his legs were amputated below his knees, and he was holding a sign: "Homeless Vet, Hungry and Lonely, Please Help." I stood up, likely too quickly, and saw black instantaneously. My head spun several times, and I braced my hand against the wall in case I fainted. "I'm good. I'm good," I reminded myself repeatedly for reassurance. I attempted to walk toward the veteran in the wheelchair to give him the twenty-dollar bill, but he was lost in the crowd. *I will see him again*, I thought as I sat back down.

I was feeling thirsty. The temperature was likely in the low nineties or high eighties, and it was extremely dry. My lips were starting to crust, further signifying that I needed some fluids. I felt something crawling on my ankles, and when I shook my leg, a small cockroach scampered across the dirty pavement, right underneath me, before it disappeared into a small crevice. I would have reacted much differently the night before. I noticed that the trivial things I previously cared about were no longer important.

I focused my attention back on the crowd. I saw what appeared to be two heterosexual Caucasian couples. What stood out about them—besides their genuine happiness—were the two red roses sticking out of their nice white bags. There was a name on the bags, but I couldn't make it out. I was sitting against the wall again and leaning over on my elbow, which was resting on my tote bag. I tried to find a comfortable position. A man from the group broke away and made a beeline toward me, carrying the fancy bag with the red roses. *Is he giving me roses? What am I going to do with roses?*

The man stopped several feet in front of me and handed me the bag. He appeared to be in his mid to late fifties, and he had a receding hairline and slight wrinkles around his eyes. He held out the bag to me.

I said, "No, thank you."

He appeared to be taken back by my response and said, "Please take it. There's food inside."

I grabbed the bag, and when I looked inside, I saw an untouched prime rib dinner.

"Thank you, sir! Thank you so much!" I put my hand over my heart to show my appreciation to the rest of the group.

"God bless," he said to me before walking over to join his group. They walked toward the stage to take in the live music. One of the women had blonde hair and was wearing white jeans and a white and red blouse. She murmured a few words to the man who slipped me the prime rib dinner before locking hands as they walked into the crowd. I couldn't help but continue looking at them. The woman, sensing my stares, looked back toward me, probably wondering what I was doing with the food. I looked down at the food, and when I looked back in their direction, I didn't see them.

I stood up to get a better view and saw that they shifted toward the very front of the stage. As a rendition of "I Love Rock 'n' Roll" blared, all four of them danced slightly off beat. They looked so happy, without a worry in the world. I was living vicariously through them, sharing in their genuine happiness. When the song ended, I was quickly reminded of my current predicament.

I sat down on the ground, a place that my lower extremities had become acquainted with. I opened the dinner bag, and to my surprise, there was another untouched prime rib meal underneath it. I sat there in amazement, before abruptly shoving them back in the bag. *I don't want anyone to jack me! I don't eat a lot of red meat, but those dinners sure look good—and I can tell they cost some money!*

Suddenly, the anxiety returned, and I needed to know the time. I have this thing about not knowing what time it is. I saw a couple walking by and said, "Excuse me! Can you please—"

They both looked at me and kept walking. *I guess they think I am begging. Oh well.*

A few minutes later, a Hispanic guy stopped in front of me. He was speaking in Spanish into his phone. I finally made eye contact with him and pointed to my wrist.

The man took a few steps toward me, placed his cell phone down to his waist, and said, "It's 12:45 a.m."

"I appreciate that. Thank you." He stared at me, raised his phone back up to his ear, and continued his conversation. I kept my eyes on him until he walked away.

Very leery of my surroundings, I remained in defensive mode. The prized possession of prime rib made me a sitting duck. I could smell the savory flavor of the meat. Each sniff made my belly growl a bit louder. I positioned my face back over the bag to get one last smell. As much as I wanted to eat them, I felt guilty knowing there were others out there who could really use the meal.

"What you gots there, boy?" I frantically looked up and realized it was Michael. I played it cool, not wanting him to know that he had startled me.

"Where have you been, man?" I said.

"Just trying, you know, to get some thangs straight, man. Shit is crazy out here, man. You gots to do what you gots to do."

I did not want to come off as judgmental and figured the best thing to do would be to not say anything. Before I responded to Michael, a disheveled man walked up to him and asked him for a smoke. Michael kindly obliged. He reached gently into his left pocket and pulled out a pack of cigarettes. The man tried to stand there as calmly as possible, but I could tell he was growing slightly impatient as Michael fidgeted through the pack, finding only a single cigarette.

As the man started to walk away, Michael yelled, "Wait, here, got one." He pulled a cigarette from his right pocket and handed it to the man.

Michael turned to me and said, "So what's in this bag, man?" He started peeking through the bag before I could answer.

"They are prime rib dinners. These couples gave them to me. I guess they thought I looked hungry."

Michael tuned me out, his eyes fixated on what was inside the bag. I could tell he was surprised by the couples' gesture, but it was apparent that Michael was eager to devour the contents. *This,* I thought, *is the right time to do something.* "Hey, those dinners are yours."

"Man, no way! Really?"

"Yes. You go ahead and have both of them—as well as the roses."

Without hesitating, Michael pulled both meals out of the bag. I thought he would simply take the meals with him, but hunger can paralyze the best of us. He ripped the plastic tops off the microwavable plates and he started eating the food with his hands.

I quickly said, "There's utensils in the bag."

"I'm good!" he shouted in an irritated voice—probably because I was disrupting his meal. Without hesitation, he used both hands to stuff as much food as he could in his mouth. I tried not to stare to avoid being rude, but I had never seen hunger like that. I eventually turned my focus to the street performers and the foot traffic in front of us.

"That was good, man. You sure you don't want this other plate." Michael looked like he was hoping I would decline.

"You go ahead. I don't like to eat this late."

"Here. Have these, man." Michael offered me a bag of half-emptied sunflower seeds.

"No, thanks. I am good," I said somewhat reluctantly. The meals looked good, but I knew I had enough money to cover breakfast and lunch.

Michael turned his focus back to the second prime rib meal, which he finished quicker than the first. "This was the best meal I had in a long time man. Thank you. I will have to pay this back to you, man.

"It's all good. You actually paid me back with your company."

"Company?" Michael asked.

"Yeah, the time you spent hanging out with me. Thank you."

"Oh yeah? All good, you know? Well, I gots to run, man, but have a good night." Michael stood up and gathered his belongings.

"Good luck on the games," I said with a smile.

"Thanks!"

We shook hands, and then he went off into the crowd.

With Michael gone, the loneliness crept back in. The foot traffic was starting to die down, and the live band stopped playing. I figured it had to be close to two thirty or three o'clock. My focus immediately turned to finding a place to sleep for the night.

I had an urge to use the restroom. I stood up, slowly this time, having learned my lesson from several hours before. The middle part of my lower back was stiff, and the backs of my legs were sore. I stretched and began to walk. After multiple steps, the pain started to subside.

I entered one of the casinos to use the restroom. I caught a few stares, but almost everyone was focused on the excitement aroused by the slot machines on the casino floor. I checked my left pocket every so often to make sure the twenty dollars was still there.

After using the restroom, I came across a Gatorade vending machine. My mouth started to water after ignoring my thirst for the past two or three hours. I slid in the twenty dollars and selected two Gatorades—Glacier Freeze and Fruit Punch—at $1.50 each. I got my change, found a seat at a slot machine, and finally relaxed comfortably for the first time.

"Excuse me, but can you please tell me what time it is?" I asked a lesbian couple as they walked by holding hands. Happy and carefree, they—along with the countless others who hurried by me—didn't notice the world just outside the casino. They didn't notice the Michaels or the veterans in electric wheelchairs. They didn't worry about when their next meal would come.

"Sure, it's, um, 3:50," one of them said cheerfully.

"Thanks!" I said loudly, but I don't think they heard me.

I couldn't believe it was almost four o'clock in the morning. The time had actually gone by fast, but I was more amazed that I still had energy. I had not been up that late in years. Sitting down at the slot machine, I didn't know where to go or what to do. I allowed another thirty minutes or so to pass before I got up. I finished one Gatorade and half of the other one. The cigarette smoke was starting to irritate my eyes. It was time to go. I walked through another cloud of cigarette smoke, just before hitting the set of double doors that led outside, and I gazed at the majesty of the desert morning sky.

FIVE

Bedtime

F REMONT STREET WAS EVEN MORE DESOLATE THAN BEFORE. The droves of people had left, but a good number still remained in downtown Las Vegas's main outdoor hub. I decided to turn the opposite way and walked toward a street corner where I found what appeared to be several other homeless folks.

I quietly sat down, minding my own business. A middle-aged White woman and a middle-aged Black man—who appeared to be together—were sitting to my immediate right. The woman was holding up a sign that I could hardly see, and they were obviously panhandling. Their clothes were extremely dirty, and a smell I couldn't describe emanated from them. Their faces looked worn and desperate. They had a small, light brown, terrier-looking dog. The dog appeared to feel the effects of homelessness as well, and her fur shared the same grime and scent. A man sitting directly behind them appeared to be in deep conversation with himself.

"Hey, man. How goes it?" the woman asked as I stretched out my legs.

"It's going. Just hanging out, you know? Where are you guys from?"

The man said, "We just got out here some days ago from Skid Row. You know about Skid Row, man?"

The woman said, "Man you don't want to end up there. Everything is bad about that place—even the rats, you know?" She pulled up the left side of her shirt to show two separate gashes right next to each other, one just above her waist and the other slightly below her rib cage. Each discolored gash was the size of a quarter. I hoped she had gone to the hospital for treatment, but then again, those were the streets.

"What happened to you?" I asked.

She exclaimed, "The rats got me. They fucking did that shit, man!"

The man said, "She OD'd, man. She OD'd on some dope, man.

She OD'd. I was out trying to get us some food that night, man, and when I came back to our little area, she was laid out, man. I thought she was dead, man. When I shook her, these fucking rats scattered—like three or four, man—and then she started to move a little."

I was in total disbelief. "Wow, that's crazy. I'm just glad you are alive and well."

"I had to get some shots, man, from the hospital, and I almost died. I should have died. Sometimes I wish I were dead."

"Don't say that, Susan!"

"Are you guys planning on going back to LA—or are you going to try to make things work here in Vegas?"

"No choice, man," Susan replied. "The row is fucked up, man. Shit, all of LA is. There's no way to afford to live there, you know?"

Another homeless man approached and whispered to Susan's partner. I suspected they were talking about drugs. As the two of them started walking away, Susan gathered their belongings.

"Are you guys leaving?" I asked, wondering if I should relocate myself.

"I don't know what's going on, but we are going. Bye. Come on, Scarlett." She picked up the dog and walked off behind the two men.

"See you later—and take care." I did not know what else to say.

They remained huddled near the sidewalk, occasionally looking in my direction. After about five minutes, they finally walked off. I could not help but think of Susan and the rats. *These streets are unforgiving.*

The guy who was talking to himself remained sitting slightly behind me. Before engaging him, I noticed several people walking past me. Groups of women in short dresses were headed to the parking garage adjacent to the street corner I was sitting on. Most people were looking straight ahead and pretending that we were not sitting there. A few noticed me, and the occasional stares actually felt pretty good.

"This is all I have—so sorry." A woman ran back and handed me a dollar bill. I had seen her walk past me a few minutes earlier. She smelled really good.

"Thank you so much. Please don't be sorry. God bless you." Feeling a rush of happiness, I could not stop smiling.

"You are welcome." She quickly pivoted and crossed the street. Just like that, she was gone to a world that was so different than mine.

I stashed the dollar bill in my pocket—right on top of the seventeen dollars that were already there. One of the dollar bills pushed to the top of my pocket and nearly fell out. Without hesitation, I unlaced my right shoe.

The man who was talking to himself suddenly became quiet and put his head down. "Stop talking to me. Stop talking to me. You so damn mean to me. Why?"

The coast is clear. I stuck the money in the middle of my shoe and put my foot inside.

"Stop talking to me. Stop talking to me! You so damn mean to me. Why?" the man said much louder.

I thought he was talking to me. Instead of getting up and walking away, I tried talking to him. I scooted backward, with my hands supporting my legs off the ground and my feet helping me to push forward, which took more energy than I anticipated. There were still five feet between us.

The man seemed to be experiencing some form of psychosis. He appeared to be in his thirties, and several gray hairs were sticking out of his patchy beard.

I was starting to feel anxious, and I did not know if it was a good idea to try to engage him. I thought, *Well, I work with mentally ill clients all the time. This should not be any different. But this is very different! I have a rapport with my clients.* "Excuse me, sir? How are you doing?"

The man started rocking back and forth with his hands planted firmly on his knees.

"Are you okay, sir?" I asked in a calmer voice.

The man stopped rocking and gave me a blank stare. I felt like his eyes were staring right through me. "What did you say to me?"

"Never mind, sir." As gently as I could, I stood up to leave the man in peace. My body was starting to let me know how late it was.

"Wait! Wait! Please, please sit," the man said excitedly.

I sat down.

"Hey, man. Sorry about that. My guard is up right now. These streets at night is something else."

"Yes, they are, and there's no need to apologize."

"So, what's your name?" he asked.

"Sheldon. What's yours?"

The man chuckled and said, "Shelby is my name. Very close to yours. Um, where are you from?"

"I've been here in Vegas for almost nine years. Originally from Southern California." I leaned to the right to get some reprieve from the hard concrete.

"I'm from Baltimore, Maryland, originally, and was then living in, um, Boston with my cousin for a couple of months, before arriving here by bus the day before yesterday."

"Wow, you came a long ways, especially by bus!"

Shelby drifted off for a few seconds, murmured something under his breath, and looked down at the concrete.

I was in no hurry, and I waited patiently for him to come back mentally.

Shelby looked back up and said, "What did you say?"

"I was just saying you came a long way."

"Oh yeah, I did." Shelby's voice began to get quieter. "I was actually staying with my cousin who took me in because I had no place to stay. I mean nowhere. I had been in the hospital back there for several weeks after trying to kill myself. I was doing better. They had me on some new meds, and they was working. I mean, I was feeling pretty darn good."

Shelby trailed off again, stared at the concrete, and started to whisper.

I couldn't make out what he was saying. I just sat there and waited for him to come back. About thirty seconds later, he came back without skipping a beat.

"Three days ago, no, four days ago or something, my cousin comes over to the couch I was sleeping on in the living room. It was early in the morning, and I was barely awake. He was like, 'Let's go to Vegas!' I got some extra cash. Let's catch the Greyhound to Vegas and gamble and stay in one of them fancy hotels." Shelby's voice began to dimmer again, the despair seemingly weighing down each word that left his mouth. "A chance to go to Vegas—and he was paying for the trip? That was a no-brainer for me."

"Yeah, I hear you on that," I said. *Given his current circumstances, that wouldn't be something I would do.*

"Um, so I am, you know, excited. So, I get dressed and packed up. I didn't have many clothes, so it did not take me long. His girlfriend or wife—I don't know what she was—drives us down to the bus stop in downtown Boston—or something like that. We waited in line at the check-in counter, or register, whatever you call it. I had to use the restroom, so when I leave and come back, my cousin is standing there, you know, just outside of the restrooms. He hands me my ticket, but he does not seem as excited as me. Probably because it's a *long* ride."

"So, you guys got on a bus at the last minute to ride across the entire country?"

"Yep, we did," Shelby said with some reluctance in his voice.

The story is still not adding up—at least not yet. "Wow, it's amazing that you guys planned a trip at the last minute like that. I guess there is excitement in being spontaneous. I will let you finish your story, my bad."

Shelby appeared to be getting irritated. "I forgot where I left off," Shelby said.

"You were saying something about your cousin handing you a ticket."

"That's right. That's right," Shelby said enthusiastically. "So, um, he hands me the ticket and says very little to me. We walk toward the bus, and I see 'Las Vegas' on the front. There's a small line of people in front of me, you know, waiting to get on. I look back once, and my cousin is talking to someone on his cell phone. So, we are standing there for a few minutes, then the line starts to move. I hand my ticket to the ticket lady, and she looks at it as I climb up the steps, you know?"

With each word, Shelby's excitement started to turn into disappointment. A scowl started to surface on his face. "I walk toward the middle of the bus since the back appeared to be taken up. I tuck my tote bag away, this same one here." Shelby pointed to a faded green tote bag. Some of the threading was sticking out, and there was a tear near the zipper. "Then I look around, and I don't see my cousin. I call out his name several times, only for the bus lady to tell me to quiet down. I tell myself he is here somewhere but can't hear me, you know?"

"Wow, Shelby. That must have been crazy!"

"That was actually the last time I saw him. He tricked me into going on the bus with him. The whole bus ride, I thought he was there with me." Shelby solemnly looked toward the ground, which appeared to be his coping mechanism.

"Shelby, I am truly sorry to hear that. How awful that must be for you."

"Man, I have nobody out here. I know nothing. I actually got stabbed last night, man."

"Wait, stabbed?"

Shelby unzipped his brownish-green jacket and stood up. "You see this?" He pointed to a bloody bandage on the right side of his chest, directly across from his heart.

"Yes, I do. What happened?"

"This dude who was camping out next to me tried to rob me. I told him I had nothing, which I really did not. He turned away, and then he stabbed me in my chest. I was freaking bleeding all over the damn place, man. I blacked out, and the next thing I know, I'm in the damn hospital. The doc stitches me up and tells me I could have died if the stab wound was closer to my heart."

I shook my head. "So, you got stabbed and left on a bus to travel across the entire country—all within a week?"

Shelby simply nodded. "I'm going to sleep now and try to go back to the shelter in the morning."

"Shelby, it was a pleasure meeting you. Be safe. As you know, these streets can be rough. Do you need anything?" A part of me hoped he would say no because I did not have much to give him.

"Naw. Nope. I'm okay. See you around." Just like that, Shelby was gone.

My heart ached for him. There appeared to be some pieces missing from the story, but I could feel his despair.

The sky was starting to lighten. *It must be after five o'clock.* I decided to walk back toward the Fremont Street Experience before I settled on my final resting spot.

A few dozen people were scattered about. The entertainers were gone, and the loud music was a faint memory. The silence was stifling. I took a few quick sips of my Gatorade to loosen the dryness in my mouth. I saw a heavyset Hispanic man passed out in a wheelchair. His clothes were worn and dirty. Nobody bothered him, including the police officers patrolling the area. I saw a young White man with no shirt on, probably no older than twenty, walking up and down and flexing his muscles. He appeared to be high on something, but nobody paid him any mind.

There was nothing left for me to do but find somewhere to sleep. I crossed several of the downtown streets, taking the same path that led me to the Fremont Street Experience. Scanning my surroundings, my paranoia remained elevated.

"Hey, honey. Hey there!" a female voice yelled from behind me.

I turned around, but I didn't see anyone.

"Hey, baby. Over here!"

I looked across the street to my left and saw two scantily dressed Black women in extremely short dresses and high heels. I nodded my head to acknowledge them, and I walked toward the corner. I probably should have ignored them and kept going, but I did not want to be rude or create any enemies in the streets.

"Why are you walking away? Come here—and we can give you a good time!"

As I approached the corner, I was tempted to cross, despite the light being red.

The two women—prostitutes, I presumed—were crossing the street in my direction.

"Hey, baby. Why you playing hard to get? Why don't you come and have some fun with us?"

As the women stood beside me, I noticed that the taller one was pregnant.

"Ladies, I have to go—but have a great night." I quickly crossed the street before the light turned green. Scanning both directions to make sure there was no oncoming traffic, I could not help but wonder what led them down this path. *Was it past trauma? Involvement in the system? A means to survival? Or a combination of all these variables?*

I walked quickly through the crosswalk and into the darkness of the tunnel. The smells of urine, feces, and trash were so strong that my eyes began to water. There were several more people sleeping on the sidewalk than earlier in the night. I walked toward the edge of the expanded sidewalk, trying not to step on anybody's legs.

A group of three men were walking down the sidewalk toward me.

"What's good? You got any blow, sherm, or bud?" one of them asked.

"Naw, man, nothing," I replied.

Another one of them asked, "You know where we could get some, homie?"

"I don't."

As I kept walking toward my destination, I reflected on what had just transpired. I had just been asked if I had drugs and had been propositioned for sex, which was likely an average night in the new world I was living in. I finally reached the top of the incline, and after looking back to make sure I wasn't being followed, I looked up at the brightening sky and laid down a few steps from a four-way intersection.

I set my tote bag down on the hard slab of concrete and rested my back against the power box. I tried my absolute best to get comfortable, sitting in various positions, but the longer I sat, the harder and more intolerable the concrete became. In desperation, I sat on top of my tote bag. Finally, some reprieve. I closed my eyes.

For thirty minutes, I could not sleep. The sun was starting to rise along with the desert heat. I gave up my pursuit for rest and noticed an unpleasant smell near me. I looked down and saw red ants crawling everywhere and a handful of crickets lurking around. I checked the bottoms of my shoes to make sure I had not stepped in bodily waste. My shoes were clear—along with the ground I was sitting on. Then, turning to my left, I saw smeared feces a few inches from my face. I quickly jumped up and gagged several times. *How did I not see this shit splatter on the power box?* I grabbed my tote bag and headed across the street to another power box.

The sun was beaming. The clock on top of a downtown hotel read

6:48 a.m. The temperature was ninety-two degrees. Immediately to my right, there was a bus stop. A middle-aged Hispanic woman was carrying several bags and a purse. She was the first person I had seen in an hour. She appeared to be going to work since she was wearing a uniform, and I envied her. I received a sense of fulfillment and meaning from working. It provided a sense of normalcy. She walked toward the bus stop, stopped, and patiently waited its arrival.

I downed the last of my Gatorade.

In front of the power box I was sitting on, there was a small concrete slab that was barely wide enough for me to lay on. I excitedly sat down and stretched out. The ground felt cool on my skin, and I was sheltered from the sun, but the reality was the ground was still hard and unforgiving, much like the world I now lived in.

I finally dozed off for a handful of minutes, and I awakened to whispers. I sat up and saw a public bus parked a few feet away. A group of Asian men and women were talking in a foreign language and looking at a map. Two of the women looked at me. I made eye contact with them, and they quickly turned away. I must have startled them. They walked off, and the smog from the moving bus rose above them.

As exhausted as I was, I felt a sense of accomplishment for being able to fall asleep—even if it was only for twenty-two minutes. I sat up and contemplated my next step. I was extremely tired, and my eyes were sore and irritated from being awake for so long. As badly as I wanted to sleep, the elements would not allow me to. I was also hungry. *Maybe I should go to the McDonald's I spotted inside one of the casinos. Today is the start of college football. I could probably hang for a little while and catch some of the games.*

SIX

Day One

AT 7:35 A.M., I STARTED MY SLOW TREK TO McDONALD'S, which was less than a quarter of a mile away. I was starting to feel weak. My lips were crusting and on the verge of cracking. My mouth was extremely dry, and my legs felt heavy. All the walking I did during the night—coupled with the prolonged periods of sitting on the hard concrete—made my thirty-nine-year-old body ache, and I had worked up quite an appetite.

As I approached the entrance of the hotel, there was surprisingly a lot of action going on. Several families were waiting for a shuttle to a tourist destination, and the men were carrying expensive cameras around their necks.

"I can't believe how hot it is out here already! We are going to cook out here!" one of the men said to his wife.

She just looked at him without saying anything.

One of their preadolescent sons ran over from the bench and said, "Dad, look! Is that where we are going?" He pointed to a billboard on the back of a pickup truck. It was a helicopter flying over the Grand Canyon.

"We are heading to the airport now to catch the helicopter," the mother said.

"I can't wait. Where's the Uber?" the kid said.

It must be nice, I thought as I continued walking to the entrance. Several bellmen passed by me without making eye contact. Usually when I walked into these hotels, they were quick to offer a smile or a "Can I help you with anything?" to get my business. *I must truly look the part since they're not even acknowledging my existence.* The doors opened automatically and effortlessly, and I entered the casino. I was surrounded by rows and rows of slot machines. Straight ahead was the lobby, and to my right—down a carpeted hallway—was the food court. I immediately saw the famous golden arches and headed in their direction.

"Sir, can I help you with something?" a stern voice asked from behind me.

Feeling irritated, I turned around and saw a younger Black man in a uniform. "No, I am fine. Thanks. Just trying to get a bite to eat."

"Are you a guest of our hotel, sir?"

"No, but I am a member of the public—and I see this is a public space, so excuse me." I was pissed. He had some nerve to approach me. All I was doing was minding my own business.

"Enjoy, sir." He stared at me before turning around and walking in the other direction.

I guess he thought I was going to just walk out of the casino after confronting me. He had made it known that I wasn't wanted there. That feeling immediately took me back to my childhood. Growing up, I was made to feel inferior by several of my White peers because of the color of my skin. I hoped I would never have to experience those feelings again because the pain ran deep. The pain was so intense that I started to hate myself. I didn't want to allow myself to go there, but I couldn't help it. If I was feeling that way, what about Michael, Shelby, and Susan—and thousands of other homeless folks? How were they feeling when their predicament was ten times worse than mine?

The line at McDonald's was twice as long as any of the other restaurants. The different food smells filled my senses and increased my appetite. Despite my dire need for food, the smells could not distract me from my irritation. It did not feel good to be unwelcome, and just to prove that point of being unwelcome in this public space, I was going to take my time. I was going to eat and relax under the nice cool air-conditioning.

There were not too many open tables. A lot of families were sitting down to get a head start on their day. As I grabbed my condiments, I spotted the last available table, which was sandwiched between families. As I sat down, I immediately pulled my food out of the bag. I quickly said grace and devoured everything in sight. I was so hungry that I could not even focus on what was going on around me. By the third breakfast sandwich, I was stable enough to focus on the beverages in front of me: a medium orange juice and a large water. With nothing but time, I sipped slowly, alternating between each drink.

"Daddy, why is the man right there sitting by himself?" an elementary-aged kid asked as he pointed in my direction. They were sitting directly to my right. There were two younger kids siting with them: a boy and a girl.

"Son, it's not nice to point. It's rude!" the kid's father said.

"Dad, why is that man sitting there by himself?" the kid asked again.

"I don't know. I don't know. Maybe he has nowhere else to go," the father said calmly as he glanced back at me.

"Can he come with us? Please!"

My head was slightly down, but I think they realized I could hear them talking. As I repositioned my feet on the floor, I stepped on a newspaper. I figured it would be the perfect distraction for me.

"Jared, no, he can't. Sorry. We don't know him. Finish your juice so we can meet Mom in the lobby."

The young boy's shoulders started to slump. He appeared to be disappointed by his father's decision. I could not help but smile to myself. Jared made me feel good. He did not know what was going on with me, but he knew something was not right—and he wanted to help me.

Before I glanced at the sports section, I looked around and saw so many smiles. Families were congregating around food before heading out on their Saturday adventures. I could not help but think about my own family. Jayden and Arianna were probably waking up right then. Nicole was likely getting ready for the day, worrying herself to death about my well-being. I wished I could be there with them, happy and smiling together like the rest of the families surrounding me.

After a few minutes, a middle-aged Black man said, "Is it okay if we borrow your chair?"

"Sure, it's all yours," I replied.

"Thank you!" The man picked up the chair and slid it to the side of a table.

Reading the newspaper was making me sleepy. The clock in the corner of the food court read 9:38. I took a few more sips of my orange juice and water before I spotted that casino employee again. My stomach started to knot up. He walked around the courtyard, and I put my head down and pretended to read the newspaper. When I looked up, he was nowhere to be found. The knots in my stomach subsided, and I felt a moment of relief. I thought about my experiences the night before and some of the heartbreaking journeys of the people.

I felt a gentle tap on my shoulder. "Sir, you can't trespass in here."

I turned abruptly, and two police officers were standing behind me. If I wasn't attracting attention before, I was doing so now. The entire food court was staring in my direction.

"I am not trespassing!" I said boldly, now feeling offended and singled out. "I will not leave. I just finished my meal, and I am now reading my paper!"

"Sir, we are going to ask you one last time. You can't remain in here. The hotel received some complaints from—"

"What? I did not do anything wrong. I bought my breakfast, and I am finishing it now. Are you telling me I can't be in here because I am homeless?"

The other officer leaned over to be closer to eye level with me. "We don't want to make a big deal about this, but you have to finish your beverages outside. We apologize, but that's what it is."

"Fine, fine. I have to go to the restroom." I was so angry that I felt my food starting to crawl up my throat. *Can they make me leave even if I am not doing anything? Were there really complaints made against me—or were they just making that up?* I grabbed my tote bag and my drinks, and I headed to the restroom inside the food court.

The police officers stood there and watched me. In the restroom, I set my beverages on the ledge above the sinks. I looked at myself in the mirror, and for the first time since the night before, I could see my bloodshot eyes. I ran some cold water over my hands and splashed it over my face to wake myself up. The cold water felt refreshing. I used the restroom and washed my hands.

An elderly White man walked in and said, "Hey, I don't know what happened, but I hate to see anyone get, you know, treated like you just did. I hope you're all right?"

"I am, sir. Thank you. Your kindness gives me strength. Good day, sir." I grabbed my beverages and walked out of the restroom.

The police officers were still waiting where I left them. In a rude way, I waved at the officers and headed out of the casino. Feeling everyone's stares, I felt insignificant—almost as irrelevant as the bubble gum stuck to the bottom of my shoe. Wait, that was an understatement. Bubble gum was usually valued by someone. Just before I exited through the automatic doors at the entrance, I crossed paths with the Black guy who had followed me earlier. He couldn't even look me in the eye. I gave him a nasty stare before walking out into the heat.

I didn't know where else to go. I quickly finished my beverages and walked a few blocks to another casino. The rays from the sun were making it more challenging to be outside. As soon as I entered the casino, the cool, crisp air from the AC hit me. I couldn't help myself. I just stood there for a few seconds, basking in the coolness, and then I proceeded to the sports book area. I wanted to sit down and watch some college football games. *I love watching college football.*

The casino was noticeably less crowded than the previous one, but the cigarette smoke was stifling. My eyes continued to burn, and I felt myself squinting. The decor in the casino had a backdrop of light blue colors, and the music playing in the background was soft and relaxing. I could have easily fallen asleep right then, standing up. Before I could, my thoughts about the incident with the police officers, resurfaced. To help with my frustration, I tried my best to reframe my thinking. *Those officers were just doing their jobs,* I told myself multiple times. After several minutes, I was able to let it go.

I found a lounge chair between the sports book and lounge area, adjacent to a bar, and I put my tote bag down next to the chair before sitting down. My body melted into the softness of the seat. Three large televisions were positioned over me, each playing a different football game. As I went back and forth between games, my eyes started to get heavy. I fought to try to keep them open. After about ten minutes, I relaxed and let them shut.

"Sir, you can't sleep in here. You must leave."

I looked up, completely startled. I could feel my heart beating rapidly.

The man staring down at me was a casino employee.

"Sorry about that." I gathered my tote bag.

When I glanced up at the television screens, all three games were nearly over. I must have been asleep for close to two hours. I headed back out into the desert heat. It was now uncomfortably hot, easily near one hundred degrees. My throat and mouth both felt dry, and I was thirsty again.

My first order of business was buying some water. I headed back to the Fremont Street Experience. I crossed two streets and walked past numerous tourists and homeless folks. I saw a homeless man holding a sign at one of the corners: "Homeless, please help me." That reminded me that I needed to make my own sign since my funds were getting low.

After walking for ten minutes, I came across a liquor store. I purchased two large cold water bottles, drinking one of them before I had a chance to pay. I did not even realize how thirsty I was until I started drinking. The top of my maroon shirt was covered with the water that missed my mouth. I had nine dollars left, which was plenty for lunch, but I would still need some money for dinner. I found a shaded area on Fremont Street, right next to where I had spent most of the previous night. I reached into my tote bag and pulled out the piece of cardboard and a black permanent marker. *What should I write?* It was hard to concentrate. It was midday in Las Vegas, during the summer, and I was running on maybe two hours of sleep. *I should write something that is going to draw the attention of others.*

After careful deliberation, I came up with this:

Homeless
Anything Will Do
Even a Smile
God Bless

It pained me to write the word "Homeless." Something about that word made me feel emotional. I thought I would never be writing a sign asking for money or food. What if homelessness was my everyday reality? Images of my family started popping into my mind. One tear, then two tears, and then four more tears landed on my cardboard sign. I stopped and looked around me to shift my focus. The vibe was noticeably different in the daytime. It was much quieter, and the crowds were smaller. There were also more families walking about—and more eyes on me.

Out of nowhere, two security guards started walking toward me. "You can't sit here. You have to keep walking," one of the security guards said in a condescending tone.

"Um look, I sat here all night last night, and nobody said one word to me. Not one word!" All the pent-up anger, sadness, and pain from the past sixteen hours spilled out.

"Sir, it's a city ordinance. You can't sit here. You can sit over there." He pointed to the middle of the walkway. "You see those circles on the ground. You can sit on those, but you have to be making something."

It dawned on me. That's why I saw random people drawing or making things in the middle of the walkway. Almost directly in front of us was a sickly looking woman with no arms; she was drawing pictures with her feet. There were several people circling around her to marvel at what she was doing. To my right, a man was painting pictures on canvases. They both had tip jars next to them.

The female security guard turned to me and said gently, "This is the last time we are going to ask you to get up." Two police officers walked over to assess the situation. The female security guard turned to the police officers, and they took a few steps back to talk in private.

I resumed my conversation with the other security officer. "So, I can stand here, but I can't sit?"

"That is correct," he said without changing his expression.

I was still feeling irritated. "So, where in the hell am I supposed to go, you know? I'm not bothering anybody. Look around. None of us is bothering anybody, you know? This whole thing is just messed up." I folded up my sign and stuffed it in my tote bag. I took the last gulp of water, and I placed the other water bottle in my tote bag.

The two police officers and the female security officer walked back over to me. The people who were passing by were stopping and staring as if something was going to happen.

One of the police officers said, "Sir, there are some places in the area you can go, such as several of the shelters. Do you know how to, um, get there?"

"Yes, I do. Thank you." I was preparing for the police officer to be confrontational, but he was actually the opposite. He was polite and helpful, which I needed right then. If he had responded in the way I was anticipating, I would have been reactive—and who knows what that would have led to! I slid my arms through the thin straps of the tote bag, and I headed toward downtown. I put my left hand in my left pant pocket to feel my nine dollars, wanting to make sure the money did not slip out of my pockets.

Since I couldn't sit down in that area, I decided to look for a shaded place to sit. I looked up at the unforgiving sun, and it was shining brighter than ever. The front and back of my shirt remained moist from my sweat. I pulled out my water bottle and began to walk.

Searching for a reprieve from the hot weather

I walked for several blocks before I finally located a corner where some random trees were offering a bit of respite from the sun. The trees hung over a large power box that was encased in a five-foot-tall wall. There was trash everywhere: torn-up cardboard boxes, ripped-up pieces of candy, and fast-food wrappers. I saw two smashed-up Happy Meals in the dirt. I walked closer and saw a mini football and a mini soccer ball surrounded by dozens of dirt-covered Legos. *Somebody has to be living here,* I thought. As I got closer, I looked over the wall and saw a person with his or her back to the wall.

I turned away and started heading up the sidewalk, disappointed that someone had beat me to the spot.

"Hey, hey?" a feminine voice yelled out.

I turned back around, but I didn't see anyone. The voice came from the encampment. I walked back over and saw a young woman breastfeeding a baby. There was also a toddler napping with his head resting on the side of the lady's lap. The woman's face was oily and leathered from the heat. Her left eye was swollen as if someone had hit her. "Were you just standing over here?"

"Yes, that was me. I was walking by to see if anyone was camping out over here, you know? I was just looking for a shady place to rest—that's all."

"Well, you scared me! You, um, you can't be walking up on people in these streets, you know what I'm saying?" The lady appeared to be irritated with me at first, but the frustration in her voice started to wane.

I said, "Look, I am sorry. I did not mean to startle you. I was just walking."

"You can't do that out here, man. Where you from?"

She caught me off guard. "I've lived here in Vegas for like eight years, but I'm originally from Cali. I have only been out here, you know, on these streets, for like a few days. It's kind of a long story, but I'm, you know, out here now just trying to survive, you know? It's real out here."

"This shit here ain't nothing compared to the streets of Chicago." She paused and adjusted her breast while still nursing her baby. "Yeah, man, I'm from the Chi, and it's no joke. I would see people killed in front of me and shit, man. That shit right there? It's crazy, man.

"Damn, that's crazy. What's your name by the way?" I hoped she did not think I was trying to pick up on her.

"My name is Betty, and yours?"

"Sheldon."

"Sheldon? That's a different name. I never heard that one before."

"Ha ha. Yeah, I get that sometimes. Can I get you guys anything? I don't have much."

"We only here until the sun goes down. My mom will be picking us up after work."

"That's still a long time to be in this heat. Why don't you go to the shelter or something?" I was confused about why she was out there in the heat, especially with children.

"Man, fuck the fucking shelter, okay? If I go in there, my boyfriend would kill me!" She started to become emotional, and she flickered her eyes to keep the tears from streaming. No matter how hard she tried, the tears flowed.

I started to think it was a domestic violence situation, but I did not want to get into her business. "Betty, are you for real when you say he would kill you?"

"Look at my fucking face! You see these tears?" she said flatly. A genuine look of fear enveloped her face, and the muscles around her neck tightened, causing her face to stretch.

The oldest boy woke up and was staring at me with a confused look. He turned to his mom and then pointed at me. "Who that man, Mammy?"

Betty turned to her son and hugged him. "He is just a friendly man I just met. Are you all done with your nap?"

He nodded, stood up, and grabbed something out of a bright green bag. The baby was probably no more than six months old and remained attached to her mother's breast. The top of her head was red from the sweltering heat.

As the baby nursed, I instantly started thinking of my wife. Nicole breastfed Jayden for several years, and she was still breastfeeding Arianna. I remember times when I would sit back and marvel at the organic nature of it all. I would see Nicole staring into their eyes, and it seemed so peaceful and calming. Breastfeeding posed its own challenges, but Betty's efforts to continue to nourish her baby, given their current circumstances, was inspiring.

I asked, "How old are your babies?"

Betty adjusted herself by sitting straight up before she answered my question. "My son, Jay, is three and will actually turn four tomorrow."

"Oh, wow!"

"My daughter is seven months old. This was her naptime. Pretty soon, we will be out of here—out of this damn heat!"

"Are you guys out here a lot?"

"What you mean?"

"Like, why are you guys out here in this heat?"

"Because my man beat my fucking ass, that's why!"

"I'm sorry. I'm sorry to hear that. Let me go now." I felt bad for asking. It elicited a lot of emotion, and I feared for my safety. *What if her "man" found us sitting there and talking? Would he think something was going on and try to harm all of us?*

"No, it's fine, man. It's complicated, you know? He gets into these rages when he is high, and he's going to fucking kill me one time, man." The tears started streaming again.

"Mammy, Mammy, what wrong? Why you crying, Mammy?" Jay ran over with a Batman figure in his hand, and the two of them embraced.

I started feeling emotional. "Betty, please take this money. It's not much. And have this water—you guys need it."

Betty started crying uncontrollably.

I walked over to her and her family, knelt down, and put my arms around them. Not knowing what to do in that moment, I started to pray. "Lord God, please wrap Your arms around Betty and her children during this difficult time. Please be their light during times of darkness and their protector during times of chaos. Please continue to spread Your love through them. In Jesus's name, we pray. Amen." I dug into my pocket, pulled out the nine dollars, and gently handed Betty the money. I put down my tote bag and handed the water to Jay. "You guys should have this. I've been blessed with this—and now I would like to bless you guys."

"Um, um, thank you, thank you!" Jay said.

"Thanks, you too kind, Shelton," the woman said. "Until we meet again."

"Yes, until we meet again." I quickly turned around and started walking. I started feeling emotional again. This very young woman was a victim of domestic violence—with a baby and a toddler—on the streets in hundred-degree weather.

Despite giving them all that I had, I wish I could have done more. It was becoming harder. I looked back toward the little encampment they had set up and squinted in the bright sun.

Jay was watching me walk away. I waved with both hands—just like I did with my own kids. He waved back to me.

My family had likely already eaten breakfast and were probably playing in the swimming pool—or maybe Jayden was watching something on his tablet, and Arianna was following Nicole around the house as she tried to clean. I wanted to hear their voices, and I wanted to let Nicole know I was safe. *I know Nicole is worried about me. About thirty hours left.*

I was walking nowhere. I didn't have a clue where to go. It seemed that homeless folks were not welcomed in any of the tourist attractions downtown. I walked back through downtown looking for a street corner where I could sit freely and panhandle for money. I could feel my lips cracking. If I opened my mouth too wide, they would likely split. My mouth was even drier, and my saliva was evaporating by the minute. I had likely burned off each calorie from breakfast. I felt a headache coming on. I needed to sit down soon; otherwise, I would pass out.

As I walked aimlessly, my thoughts kept shifting between the beautiful people and my need for a place to go. Their stories stayed with me, which made me feel even more helpless. *I want to help them all because that's my nature. It's who I am and what I do for a living. Folks are hurting out here, and it is going to take more than a Band-Aid to heal these wounds.*

I finally approached a corner in the heart of downtown that seemed safe. It was the same corner where I sat uninterrupted the night before. The busy corner was surprisingly empty, but the adjoining sidewalk was bustling with people. There was also a hint of shade, which I desperately needed. I slowly put my tote bag down on the ground and felt a tap on my back. I turned around.

A small middle-aged Asian man was looking at me. He was surrounded by a group of men and women.

"Excuse me please, can you tell us where the Fremont Street thing is? It's, um, um, big canopy thing."

"It's that way." I stretched out my right arm and pointed.

"Thank you. Thank you."

They all nodded and bowed in unison. Several of them waved to me, and I nodded back, not feeling in the mood to be social. Several of them had expensive cameras. *One of those cameras has more value than my life—at least that's what I feel based on the treatment I received.*

I guessed it was likely between two o'clock and three o'clock. My butt finally touched the concrete, and the heat immediately pierced my hand-me-down jeans. The sun radiated from my knees to my feet with my stretched legs. I pulled my sign out of my tote bag and held it. My head was pounding. Dozens of people continued to walk past as if I didn't exist. From time to time, a tourist would glance my way and try to make sense of my sign.

As I sat, I could feel the temperature rising.

"Hey, man, this is all I got man." A Black man walked up from behind me, briefly startling me, and handed me a one-dollar bill. As he leaned over, two gold chains slipped out from underneath his collar. He was dressed in a neatly pressed gray designer suit. He looked like a pastor, and I could tell he was itching to get out of the Las Vegas heat.

"Thank you. Thank you so much," I said. *One dollar, I had discovered, goes a long way when you're in survival mode.*

"I will get you more the next time. God bless you, man."

"God bless you too," I replied, but the man was already gone. I looked at the crinkled dollar bill that was mere change to the man, and I remembered how I kept change in the center console of my car, ignorant of the value that it held. On that day, I held on to that dollar bill, squeezed tightly in my hands, as if my life depended on it.

I was convinced the hot concrete was leaving first-degree burns on my legs and buttocks. Every twenty-five to thirty-five seconds, I shifted from lying down to sitting up to briefly standing. Shifting my weight from one leg to the other offered some reprieve. I noticed the cockroaches crawling on me in a futile effort to escape the heat. *Last night, I had too much pride to let them climb on me, but I don't care anymore.*

Panhandling for money

I tried to spit, but nothing came out. I needed to get some fluids, but from where—and with what? A dollar wouldn't be enough. Feeling too fatigued to hold my sign, I gently placed it up against my tote bag in a position that others could see. I spotted an empty water cup behind me that I could use to hold change. I stuck the dollar bill in the cup, sat down on the hot concrete, and placed my head between my legs.

"Hi, is it okay if I sit here?"

I looked up, and a middle-aged Caucasian woman was standing over me with bags of clothes and what looked like all her belongings. Her skin was leathered and dry. She looked very fragile and weak, and her cheeks were slightly sunken. Her blue jeans had holes and were stained. Her red shirt was partly covered by a sleeveless jean jacket that matched her pants.

"I don't own this corner. Please ... be my guest." I extended my right arm toward the ground in an attempt to usher her to the space. Considering how terrible I was feeling, I figured a little company wouldn't hurt.

"Thank you so kindly." She put down her bags, pulled out a blanket, and sat on it. "So, do you stay around these parts?"

"Yeah, I stay not too far from here. I came over here for a break from the sun. My name is, um, Sheldon."

"That's an interesting name. Sheldon? I don't think I've ever met anyone with that name. My name is Sandy. I am from the great state of Texas."

"Texas? Wow, that's a long way away. How long have you been in Vegas?"

"I've been here for, like, several weeks or so. My great state could not do anything for me—so here I am. I have a friend who lived here, but he died last week in his sleep. I couldn't afford to take over his rent, so with nowhere to go, here I am." Sandy was noticeably upbeat considering her circumstances.

"I am sorry for your loss."

"Yeah, it sucks. George was a good man. I will go back to the shelter tonight. I can't really work because I am sick. I basically live off my Social Security."

"So, you are—"

"Sick? Yes, I am sick. I actually don't have much time to live. I was diagnosed with stage-4 breast cancer a year or so ago. It has spread throughout my body as well as to several organs."

My heart wept. I tried my best to be genuine and as present as possible. "I am so sorry, Sandy. Um, I don't really know what to say, you know? I am just so sorry you have to go through what you are going through out here."

"Please, Shelton, don't be sorry for me. I am really okay. I have put this whole thing into God's hands, and I finally have peace. I went through my anger and grief period, and that was hard, you know? I think the hardest thing has been how people treat you once you have a certain label."

Sandy's strength was touching. Hearing her journey made me quickly forget how dehydrated I was. "I can't obviously know what you are experiencing, but I understand what it is to be labeled and treated differently because of that label."

"Shelton, Shelton, your lips are bleeding!" Sandy yelled in an animated voice, mispronouncing my name.

Feeling somewhat indifferent, I said, "They are?" I felt a burning sensation on my bottom and top lips, but I did not think too much of it.

"You must be dehydrated. Here … have this water." Sandy grabbed an unopened bottle of water out of one of her bags, twisted the cap off, and graciously handed it to me.

"Thank you, Sandy." I grabbed the bottle, which felt more like a cup of hot coffee, and chugged the water as fast as I could.

"Here … have another one." Sandy reached into another bag.

Several pairs of her underwear fell on the ground, and she stuffed them back into the bag. She handed me another water bottle and said, "You did *not* see that."

"No, I did not see anything. Thank you for the water. You are a lifesaver. Is this your last water?"

"I don't know," she said.

"Well, I don't want to drink it if this is your last water bottle. It's hot out here, and this heat is nothing to play with."

"Shelton, please drink the water. I will be fine either way. God is with me."

If I continued to resist, she would just persist. I guzzled the second water bottle almost as quickly as the first one.

"I think you set the record for fastest person to drink two hot bottles of water!" She chuckled.

"That's a good one, Sandy!" The pressure in my head was already starting to dissipate. I still felt out of it, but my mouth and my lips were not as dry. "So, how were you treated when you were diagnosed with, um, cancer?"

Sandy looked down at the ground and then back up before glancing at some of the people walking past us. She seemed to be in deep thought, carefully deciding how to answer my question. She finally looked me in the eyes and said, "Just put it like this, you really learn who truly cares about you when you go through adversity, and your situation, like, um, your situation that you are now in makes things less convenient for them."

"I hear what you are saying," I said.

"I worked for this company for eight years in the sales department. All I know is sales, and when they found out my diagnosis, they tried pushing me out. I missed a lot of days due to my chemo treatments, but I was loyal, man. Even the days when I did not feel like going in because of being sick and weak from the chemo, I still went in.

I started getting written up, which turned to discipline—and I eventually got let go."

"Wasn't there any recourse for that? I mean, was there any way to fight back against how they were treating you?" I shifted from side to side to try to cool my legs.

Shaking her head, Sandy said, "Nope—not a darn thing. Believe me, I tried and everything. I even retained an attorney, who I still owe money to, and there were some grounds for a lawsuit, but the money and energy that would have taken were not worth it to me. So, I had to stop fighting the good fight."

"Wow, Sandy. I just hate to hear how you were treated."

"Well, that's life, you know? The good thing that came out of it was that I came to know the Lord. I dedicated my life to Him by getting baptized a few months ago. Now, I feel Him with me, and I am looking forward to reaching that number one destination: heaven."

"Well, Amen to that, Sandy."

"So, despite how sick I am, I am at the most peace. Right after my diagnosis, I was so scared, you know? And then that fear turned into a deep depression. I numbed myself with alcohol, but that just made me feel worse."

I put on my therapy hat and replied, "Unfortunately, that's what substances do. They allow people to briefly forget about their predicaments. However, the pain usually always remains if other healthier mechanisms are not adopted."

"You are right," Sandy exclaimed. "I want to learn more about you, but I am afraid that I have to go get in line at the shelter soon. I came over here for a bite to eat." Sandy checked the time on her watch and stood up. She started gathering herself, including the blanket she was sitting on.

"What time do you have?" I asked.

"It's, um, 4:33."

"Thank you!" I said. Finding out the time, when you have very little idea of it, was refreshing. It was also a mental game that allowed me to count down the moments until I could see my family.

"Shelton, it has been a pleasure," she said. "Be safe out here—and God bless you."

"Thanks, Sandy, for your company and your testimony."

She placed three bags of clothing and her hygiene bag in each hand and walked off. She looked back at me and waved before disappearing.

I already miss Sandy. Despite what she is dealing with physically, she saw to it that I was comforted and taken care of. She saw that I was dehydrated and in need of water, and she gave me all that she had. Her generosity and testimony did something to me. The discomfort I was experiencing vanished—at least for the time being. Her positive attitude and selflessness, while literally being on her deathbed, encouraged me. The only thing I want to think about is her.

I quickly switched my attention from Sandy to my own pressing needs. I was still quite thirsty and very hungry, but I only had one dollar to my name. I repositioned myself on the hot concrete with the sign in my lap. I hoped people would be able to see the sign and offer me enough spare change to buy a meal to last me through the night.

Person after person walked by. Several people glanced at me and then glanced at the sign before walking off. Others walked past without even looking in my direction, which brought pain to my heart. *How can people ignore me despite the despair apparent before their very eyes?*

After thirty minutes or so, a Hispanic family walked past me: a mother, father, two daughters, likely ages five and ten, and a boy who was likely six or seven. As the family passed me, the kids couldn't help but stare. The boy's level of curiosity mirrored that of my son. He was trailing behind the rest of his family, seemingly trying to process why I was sitting on the corner.

"Jose, come now!" the father yelled back at the boy.

Jose did not budge. He continued to stare in a curious way.

I decided to acknowledge the boy by waving.

He waved back before running to catch up to his family.

I saw the boy's mother talking to him, and I could tell she was saying something about me. What empathy the boy was exhibiting at such a young age.

Three hours had passed, and I still had only one dollar. I needed to find a different spot—or go without food. The shelter would be a last option, but I didn't want to risk running into someone I might know, thus negating all that I had sacrificed. I decided to move.

Before I stood up, I put down my sign and grabbed my tote bag.

Two women stopped at the corner and waited to cross the street. One of the women looked at me, and we made eye contact. To my dismay, she turned forward and continued waiting for the streetlight to turn so she could cross the street. I was hopeful that she might bless me with some change, but I was wrong. The light turned green, and the two women started to cross. To my surprise, the woman I made eye contact turned around and walked back toward me.

"Hi, there. I hope you are doing okay. I could not help but see you sitting over here." The woman was beautiful and nicely dressed. Her perfume smelled expensive. She reached into her purse and handed me a twenty-dollar bill.

"You don't have to do this, but thank you. Thank you so much!"

"It's the least I could do. Please take care of yourself. Bye-bye." She started to walk back to the corner to join the other woman.

"Thanks again!" *Why me? I am grateful, but what about my plight drew her to me? Was it being in the right place at the right time? Did my obvious discomfort elicit empathy in her?*

I felt so appreciative and blessed. I had enough money for at least two meals and enough water to keep hydrated. I clenched the twenty-dollar bill in my right hand, strapped on my tote bag, and headed to a fish taco eatery that I was craving.

I could smell the battered fish before I even entered the establishment. I was so hungry that my stomach was cramping. After placing my order, I found a table in front of the television that was airing the Michigan versus Notre Dame football game. The eatery was packed, and just about every table occupied. My order was ready, and I inhaled my three fish tacos with a side of beans and rice, alternating sips of my lemonade and water.

After I finished my meal, I stuck around—watching most of the football game and filling my bladder with plenty of water. With two younger kids, I never would have been able to watch the game without being interrupted, so this was a treat. I missed my little guys. I would trade all the noise and distractions of the game to be with them. I had a little less than ten dollars remaining, which was plenty for breakfast in the morning.

Thinking I could get through the day with one meal and several bottles of water and Gatorade, I headed out of the eatery. The sun was starting to set, and the sky was darkening. My stomach was full, and I was extremely tired. I was hopeful that I could sleep that night. I headed back to the slab of concrete in front of the power box where I briefly fell asleep that morning.

In the dark tunnel under the bridge, a tall man was jogging in my direction. "The stars are falling down. Run, run, run, run!" He kept looking back at me as he ran.

I kept looking back to make sure he didn't try to do something. I could hear his voice echoing in the tunnel until he finally disappeared. I finally made it out of the tunnel, and my resting spot was within reach.

"Oh shit!" I nearly fell over a sleeping man's leg in the middle of the sidewalk. It scared the crap out of me. I did not even see him by the opening of the tunnel. "I'm so sorry, sir."

The man did not budge.

I gently shook him to make sure he was still alive. I could smell the strong odor of alcohol. I shook him again.

He moved slightly, opened one of his eyes, and yelled, "Get away from me!"

"Okay, okay. I was just checking to make sure you were okay."

"Leave me alone!" he shouted again.

I left the man where he was and kept walking until I arrived at my resting spot, which was a few hundred feet away. *I hope no one tried to do anything to him,* I thought. I sat on top of the green power box and stared up into the dark summer night. I couldn't help but marvel at the bright starts that pierced the sky. I saw red lights occasionally moving above me. *They must be tour helicopters providing tourists aerial views of the Strip.*

I glanced up to my right for the time and temperature. It was 8:08 p.m. and ninety-six degrees. As I reflected on the day, I started feeling emotional. My throat started to knot up. *What is going on with me?* A flood of tears started streaming down my face. I couldn't help but think about how I was treated at the casino that morning, the way people stared, the way people made me feel like I was invisible, and the stories of all the people I was fortunate to meet. It all hit me at once. I cried and I cried. *Shoot, I haven't cried like this since the last time I played basketball as a high school senior, which was in 1997.*

After what felt like an eternity, I wiped the last of the tears with my forearm. Feeling overwhelmingly tired, I moved off the power box and onto the concrete slab. I took off my tote bag and used it as a makeshift pillow. I checked my surroundings one last time. It was eerily quiet—with only the occasional car passing by. I rested my head on my tote bag and closed my eyes.

SEVEN

The Second Night

BEING AWAKENED BY A CAR THAT WAS BLASTING MUSIC several feet in front of me was probably one of the most traumatic things I'd ever experienced. I was in such a deep sleep that, for a second, I forgot where I was—or even what I was doing. It took several minutes to realize what was going on. I sat up, stared at the row of cars in front of me, and wiped away the drool that had puddled on the left side of my face. The streets were busy after all it was a Saturday night on a holiday weekend. I sat on top of the green power box and looked at the clock on top of the casino: 9:38. I had been asleep for a little over an hour. *I could definitely use eight or nine more hours, but that is not going to happen while I am out here.*

I decided to head back to the Fremont Street Experience to buy some time. I walked back up the tunnel, stepping over and around some of the homeless people who were sleeping there. A few blocks later, I noticed the droves of people canvasing the downtown streets. It was definitely more crowded than the previous night.

When I finally made it to the Fremont Street Experience, there was hardly any room to walk without bumping into someone. Live music was blaring from the stage, and background music was flowing from the overhead speakers. The sounds were more amplified than the previous night. I also noticed a stronger law enforcement presence. I walked over to my usual spot, but it was occupied by a group of tourists. Instead of sitting, I leaned against the wall. After several minutes, they walked away—and there was finally enough space to sit down.

After about five minutes, a police officer walked up to me and said, "Excuse me, sir, but you are not permitted to sit here. You can stand here, but you can't sit here."

Already knowing what the ordinance was, I still decided to be difficult. "I actually sat in this same place for most of the night last night, and not one police officer said I could not sit here. Now, why is that?" I rose to my feet.

"I can't answer that. Those who remain seated after being issued a warning will be cited." As he spoke, two other police officers walked over, somewhat causing a scene, and people in the area stopped to take a peek.

"Wow, this is unbelievable. It wouldn't even be an issue if you guys were consistent. I actually feel like I am being targeted, but whatever. I will just stand then."

"Thank you for your cooperation, sir," the initial police officer said.

As they started walking away, one of the police officers—who happened to be Black—turned to me and said, "Why are you here to begin with? Shouldn't you be at one of the shelters?"

Feeling even more targeted and agitated, I decided to speak my mind. "Listen, who are you to tell me where I should be or what I should be doing?"

The two other officers walked back over.

I said, "You guys need to talk to him about how to respect people! Why don't you tell them what you just asked me!" I noticed my voice projecting louder over the blaring noise.

The officer said, "Sir, you need to settle down—or we will need to take you in!"

"For what? I'm not doing anything. Your partner right here is the one who needs to be checked."

"Sir, that's enough! If I have to tell you again, I will arrest and book you!"

"Okay. I am done. Have a nice night," I said as I walked away. *If I stay there, I will likely go to jail. That officer really got me riled up. He offended me, and I reacted. I know you are not supposed to react to a police officer, but I felt obligated to say something. It was completely uncalled for.* Walking away, I felt more eyes on me. I looked back and saw the three police officers watching me walk away.

Feeling slightly thirsty, I walked inside one of the casinos to use the restroom and purchase a Gatorade from the vending machine. Sipping my strawberry Gatorade, I sat down at one of the quarter slot machines.

A man stopped in front of me and stared me up and down, paying close attention to my shoes. His face gave a look of empathy, and then he abruptly walked away. I looked down at my shoes and saw the sides were covered with white residue. That was interesting. A telltale sign I had been sleeping on the streets.

I walked back to my usual spot on the corner. The police were gone, and I saw no tourists either. I put down my tote bag and sat on the familiar concrete.

A lady with uncombed, matted hair and tattered clothing approached me and said, "You gots some bud, dude?"

"Sorry, I don't do that."

"You gots some blow? I need some bad!"

"I don't have any of that either. You are more than welcome to sit and chat if you like."

"Ha! I ain't sitting with you!" The lady quickly ran across the street toward another group of people, likely asking the same question. I noticed one of the men hand her something white. She grabbed what appeared to be a cigarette before running quickly away in the opposite direction.

I sat back in my space. Several bugs crawled on my legs, likely cockroaches, but it was hard to tell because it was dark. People of all ages and many different races were walking up and down the sidewalk. It was nearing midnight, and I was starting to feel sleepy again. I was probably functioning on a little more than two hours of sleep, including my recent nap. I pulled out my Gatorade and took my last sips for the night. The bottle was halfway full. I would drink the rest in the morning.

"Excuse me, but you can't sit here. It is private property," said a tall, muscular Polynesian man with a security shirt and a bulletproof vest. He was carrying a firearm.

"That's weird. I actually sat in this same corner last night and for several hours today. You can even check your cameras if you think I am not being honest." I was calmer this time around. He was respectful in how he approached me, and I did not want to cause any more trouble.

"Yeah, depending on who is patrolling, they may say you can sit here as long as you don't go to sleep, but our policy is that nobody can sit here or lie down here—no matter what time of day it is."

"I understand. It's just interesting how I was able to chill here and on the Fremont Street Experience without anyone saying a single word to me. All of a sudden, Saturday rolls around—and I am no longer welcome to sit anywhere down here?"

"I don't know what else to say. Have you checked out any of the shelters?"

"Yeah. I am familiar with them, but I don't want to wait in those long lines in the heat."

"Well, have a good night. I'm sorry to be a pain in the ass, but I have a job to do."

When the security guard started walking away, I stood up and put on my tote bag. "It's all good. I understand. Good night to you as well."

Back at the Fremont Street Experience, I saw the same police officers from the night before. I decided to leave, but I had nowhere to go. I was not ready to head to my rest stop. There were likely a lot of cars passing through since it was early. I thought of the freeway bypasses. It was a place I frequented when passing out food and hygiene kits to the people there.

I started my trek away from the hustle and bustle that a downtown Saturday night drew to the quiet and dark streets of the homeless corridor. I was one of a few people walking around. It appeared that almost everyone was sleeping.

As I neared one of the shelters, masses of people were sleeping on the sidewalks in sleeping bags, tents, or on the concrete. Several of the streetlights were not working, and it was dark. I saw one man standing and talking to himself. As I passed him on the other side of the street, he stopped talking and watched me walk by. After I passed him, I looked back and saw him step off the curb and walk toward the middle of the street. I could see him talking to himself again, but he was facing me and talking directly to me.

I kept walking and picked up my pace. I could see the bypass in the distance. Looking back over my shoulder, I no longer saw him standing there. I crossed the street just before the bypass and found an open space. I decided to park myself for the time being. I took off my tote bag and sat down with my back against the wall. I didn't feel comfortable lying down because the sidewalk was dirty.

Jumping up, I felt several large cockroaches crawling on my legs and on my back. I knocked them off by frantically hitting myself. I felt something crawling on my shoulder, near my neck, and using a sweeping motion, I knocked whatever it was off of me. When I looked down at the ground, I could see a large brown spider. I immediately stepped on it, grabbed my tote bag, and shook it several times to ensure there were no insects trying to come along for a ride.

Where should I go now? I realized the only safe place I could go without being bothered by law enforcement or awakened by bugs was where it all began. I started to make the half-mile walk back to the green power box. My legs were feeling increasingly fatigued, and my eyes were starting to feel irritated. I stopped at a red light, and the streets were quiet. The light seemed to not want to turn green. Growing impatient, I crossed the street. My eyes felt heavier and heavier as if they wanted to close shut. I was beyond tired. I could see the green power box two blocks ahead.

As I inched closer, I saw something standing in the middle of the street. As I got closer, I saw that it was the same guy from a few minutes earlier. He was wearing a black plaid sweater, black pants, and a black beanie. He was barefoot. He said, "The devil is coming for us right now!"

My inclination was to ignore what he said and keep walking, but I did not trust him—and he was standing close to the spot I had claimed as my own.

"When will the devil be here?" I asked, anticipating an irrational response.

"The devil is here amongst us!" The man pointed all around him. "He is talking to me right now."

"What is he telling you? I want to know!"

"He tells me that you come from the world of evil and that I need to convince you not to go back."

"I have to go back since it's, um, the only world I know. If I don't go back, I will never get to see my family." *This is starting to get a little weird. This man is speaking some truth to me.*

"If you go back, you must tell the people about this world." The man stared into my face.

When I made eye contact with the man, I only saw white. There were no pupils. I asked, "What do I say to them?"

He looked around as if to ensure nobody else was listening and said, "That is for you to figure out." He started walking down the street.

I was so confused, and I tried to process that interaction. When I looked back to see where the man was headed, he was nowhere to be found. *That's weird! I know he did not just disappear. What is going on?* I took a few more steps toward my destination. When I looked back again, there was nothing but darkness.

When I looked forward, the man was standing in front of the green power box. *What the hell? I'm going to have to fight this guy.*

Wait, how did he get from behind me without me knowing? I didn't have the energy to run away from him, but I had a little fight left to defend myself. I just hoped that he did not have a shank. I started walking toward the man, preparing for the worst. One ... two ... three steps, and the man was gone! *What the fuck?* I didn't normally use profanity, but I was terrified! I arrived at the power box, and there was no one to be found. I looked back again. Nothing! *Where did he go? Am I tripping? I must be tripping. Damn, I've never experienced anything like this.* I still didn't know if my mind was playing tricks on me—or if someone really was lurking out there. I was so fatigued, and my level of concern was dwindling as each minute passed.

I was finally at the green power box. My connection to the power box was becoming more significant with each visit. When I was younger, a similar green power box was across the street from my house. All the neighborhood kids would congregate around the power box to laugh, tell jokes, and share stories. I would meet by best friend there before walking to school in the morning. It was a reminder of a time when life seemed so easy. Now, I was homeless, sitting at a green power box, hundreds of miles away and decades later, and it would provide me the same comfort. That must have been why I kept going back.

I pulled out the warm Gatorade bottle and finished what was left. I glanced up at the clock above the hotel: 4:28. No way! It was midnight an hour or so ago. The temperature was eighty-eight degrees, but it seemed a lot cooler with the absence of the sun. My eyes started to feel heavy again. *I hope I can finally sleep.* I hopped off the green power box and noticed several crickets invading my space. I tried my best to kick them away, but trying to kick a cricket is like trying to catch a fish with no hook. After ten minutes of cricket kicking, I finally stopped and sat down on the concrete slab. I dozed off a few times before I started imagining a scorpion invading my space. My mind was operating in protective mode, and with every sound or movement I felt, I went into fight-or-flight.

I tried resting my head on my tote bag again. As I started to close my eyes, someone across the street started coughing uncontrollably. I sat up to see what was going on. I saw a man in a squatted position with his pants pulled down. Before I could turn away, a liquid stream of diarrhea came gushing out from underneath him. I gagged several times.

Another man was sitting against a large power box, only a few feet from the man who was using his personal restroom. The men must have known each other because they were talking. I looked over at the man who was pooping. He appeared to be done—and then he took his hand and scooped out what remained. I couldn't help but gag again. Feeling completely nauseous and grossed out, I tried my best to distract myself, hoping that would alleviate the nausea, but it continued to linger.

When I finally rested my head on my makeshift pillow, I felt something crawling on my leg again—but I couldn't muster enough energy to see what it was. I finally closed my eyes.

EIGHT

The Final Day

WHEN I WOKE UP, IT WAS MORNING. I COULD NOT STOP thinking about my family. I missed them so much. I just needed to get through the day, and I would be able to see them. I couldn't stop staring at the family picture that my wife had slipped into my tote bag. I knew she had to be a nervous wreck right then, not knowing what was happening to me. I immediately shifted my focus on the final eight hours of my homeless experience.

It was close to noon. I hadn't eaten anything, but I didn't have much of an appetite. Maybe it was due to the lack of sleep or the adverse weather conditions. My lips were extremely dry, and any sudden movements of my mouth would likely cause several splits in my lips. I stopped by a mini-mart and purchased two thirty-two-ounce bottles of water, leaving me with four dollars, which was barely enough for a meal.

I decided to walk almost a mile to the park where I began my journey. With large, shade-providing trees, I could get away from the heat. I sipped on my water and tried to preserve it. As I approached the park, I saw multiple homeless people hanging out. One man was using a water fountain as a makeshift shower. He was bathing himself from his waist up. It looked like he made a hole in the bottom of a soda can to create water pressure. *What a clever idea,* I thought.

I found a nice resting spot between two large trees. As I sat down, I could feel the coolness of the grass. I scanned the park to make sure nothing sketchy was taking place. I rested my head against my tote bag and closed my eyes for a much-needed nap.

The insects crawling on me woke me up every few minutes. I sat up and looked at the sun. Its rays were piercing through an opening between several branches. I guessed it was around two o'clock.

Two Hispanic men entered the park and started walking toward me. They looked fairly clean cut and certainly didn't appear to be from around there. They were both wearing brown work boots, blue jeans, and T-shirts. I couldn't help but feel a little nervous. They sat down on a bench a few feet in front in me and stared at me for about twenty minutes. One would look back at me before turning to the other and talking. Their suspiciousness was unnerving.

Are they going to try to rob or hurt me? Do I look familiar to them? If they wanted to do something to me, it was the perfect time because there were no witnesses besides another man passed out on a bench. He was shirtless and surrounded by pigeons.

I put my head down between my legs, bowed my head, and closed my eyes. "Dear Jesus, please continue to be with me during this time. I thank You for your protection and the favor You have shown me. Please continue to use me to be a voice for the voiceless, and lastly, to get home safely to my family. Amen."

I felt calmer after praying. I looked in the direction of the two men, and they remained seated in their same positions. They actually stopped looking back at me, but I kept my eyes fixed on them just in case. I felt like they were plotting something. I clenched my tote bag just in case I had to run or defend myself. I started to feel lightheaded. I took a few gulps from one of my water bottles, which was almost empty. I could feel the adrenaline racing through my body. My heart was pumping, sweat was dripping all over my body, and my fatigue had dissipated.

The shorter man stood up and walked toward me. "Do you have any smokes?" he asked from about ten feet away.

"Sorry, I don't have any." I tried not to show how nervous I was.

He took a few steps closer, but he was still far enough away that I didn't feel threatened.

"Damn, nobody around here has a smoke!"

"Sorry, man. I don't even smoke to be honest. I'm just chilling out here to get away from this, um, sun, you know?"

"It's all good, bro. My cousin and I just were looking for a smoke so we can pass some time, you know what I am saying?" He made himself comfortable and sat down across from me.

"Sure, I get it. Do you and your cousin stay around here?"

"Naw, bro. We live at the shelter around the corner. We been staying there for two weeks now. We usually kick it at this park for several hours before we have to get in line to secure a bed, you know?"

"Oh, I see."

"Yeah, we saw you walk inside the park and hoped you had some smokes or something, you know?"

"You saw me where?" I asked, trying to make sure they were not following me.

"We saw you as you walked through the park. We were sitting along that fence over there. You looked new to these parts. So, we figured to hit you up, you know?"

"I see. Yeah, I'm not from around here. I fell on some tough times recently and have been camping out here the past two days, you know? Man, it's tough out here. I don't know how people do it for weeks, months, even years, you know?" I tried my best to keep the conversation light. I didn't want to lie and fabricate some elaborate story about what had landed me on the streets.

"Yeah, it sucks out here!" He waved over to his cousin.

The cousin stood up slowly, limped over, and sat down across from me. "What's up?"

"I'm just chilling," I responded. "What's your names?"

"Oh!" The shorter cousin reached out his hand and said, "I'm Cesar, and that's Ernesto."

I shook their hands. "And I'm Sheldon."

Ernesto looked at Cesar and then looked at me in amazement. "You don't look like a Sheldon. I never heard that name before."

"Yeah, I get that all the time. So, how did you guys end up here?"

Cesar turned to me and said, "It's a long story, to be honest, but I will give you the short since you asked."

Ernesto said, "Which version of the short are you going to give?"

"Whatever comes to me," Cesar said with a wry smile. "All I know is we hit rock bottom, and we hit it quick, man. My cousin was laid off from his job almost a year ago or so. He got depressed and all and started drinking. His wife left him after several months."

Ernesto stood up and walked off to the other side of the park.

"Is he okay?" I asked.

"Yeah, this whole thing has been harder on him, I think, than me. He has never forgiven his lady for leaving him. Us Mexicans are loyal, and that was, man, a huge blow to him. Because he could not afford the rent, he had to move in with me. Then I lost my job because my cousin lost it one day. He calls me at work and was like, 'Yo, I'm going to do it!'

"I knew he was going to try to kill himself because he tried doing it before. I rushed home without telling my boss, and the good thing was I made it home in time. The bad is I lost my job."

"Man, Cesar, sorry to hear that. Definitely an unfortunate set of circumstances."

"But you know what? I would do the same thing again if I had to. If I got home a few minutes after I did, my cousin would not be here right now, you know?" Tears started flooding his eyes.

My eyes started to tear as well. Here we were, two men in a park, in an impoverished neighborhood, who barely knew each other, able to show some vulnerability. "I think that's great what you did, Cesar. You put family first over everything else. Man, I give you a lot of respect for that."

"Really, it was a no-brainer for me. His life, or anyone's life, is more important. That job was no longer important to me for them to fire me just like that. They had to do what they had to do—so that's what it is."

I said, "So, how did you guys end up in the shelter?"

Ernesto started walking back toward us.

"Ah man, that's another long one. The short version is that I ended up getting evicted from my apartment because I could not pay the rent. I am an electrician, and I guess that there are a lot of electricians in this city because I could not find work for the longest time. Most of our family lives in Cali, and the family we do have here are druggies—and I did not want anything to do with them, man. So, a neighbor told me about the shelter as a temporary option, and several days turned to several weeks." Cesar kept shaking his head.

When Ernesto sat down, his eyes were slightly swollen from crying.

"Are you good, homie?" Cesar grabbed the top of Ernesto's shoulder and slightly shook it.

Ernesto smiled briefly before putting his head down.

I reached into my tote bag. "Hey … please take this water."

Cesar said, "Thanks, but we are good. We got to get in line soon so we get a bed."

"No, please have this water. You guys share it." Even though it was my last one, I felt compelled to let them have it. They would be standing in line in the hot sun, and the water would be useful. I could make do under the shade—at least, I hoped I could.

Cesar took the water and said, "Man, thank you so much for this!" He took a few gulps and handed the water bottle to Ernesto.

I was dumbfounded. The least I could do was offer them my water and some words of encouragement. "You guys have fallen on some tough times, but you guys got this. I know that you both will get back on your feet real soon, and all this will soon be behind you."

Ernesto handed the water back to Cesar. He looked like he was trying to find the right words to say. He looked toward Cesar, almost for encouragement, and said, "You are right, man. We can only go up from here. But, you know, I have a question for you."

My heart started beating fast. *They must have me figured out. My cover is blown.* "Sure, what's your question?"

Ernesto said, "Man, I will be honest with you. If you weren't the way you are—like, if you weren't cool and shit—we was going to rob you!"

Surprised, I could only chuckle.

"What the hell!" Cesar yelled. "Why the hell did you even say that? That was so stupid!"

"My bad, but I thought he should know."

I said, "Um, well, thank you, um, for telling me that. I'm sure glad you guys did not try to rob me!"

We all started laughing—even Cesar.

"I don't have much, so it would have been a complete waste of time, but it would have been quite the experience."

"It's cool," Cesar replied.

"I'm just curious. Why me?"

Cesar said, "The idea was all mine. We did not think you were from around here. You look like an outsider, you know?

Ernesto said, "Look, we gots to go get in line at the shelter. It's almost three thirty."

"Shit, let's go!" Cesar took a quick swig of the water.

"Listen, I will pray each day for you guys that you are able to get back on your feet very soon."

"Thank you. Thank you!" they both said in unison.

I stood up to shake their hands, and they were off. *It is a peculiar feeling to shake the hands of people who wanted to rob you moments earlier. It's mystifying how intuition can be spot on. I knew something was odd about them all along, but I completely ignored it. I will never forget them.*

I started thinking about how much time I had left. In a little more than four hours, I would see my family. I was exhilarated, but I decided to temper my excitement. I still had a long time to go. I needed to busy myself, but how?

An older man and a frail younger woman walked into the park and sat on the steps by the playground. I tried not to stare, but I couldn't help myself. The woman was shaking. The man was trying to hold her body in place, but she kept shaking. Her body was seizing uncontrollably and jerking back and forth and from side to side. There was no emotion on her face, and her eyes looked as though they were not connected to her body. The man looked over at me to see if I was watching. I drank the remaining drops of my water; the heat was scorching my body. The shade had all but left my little area. I decided to walk over to an empty bench on the other side of the park. Several trees over the bench provided some shade.

As I walked closer to the bench, it appeared that the man was trying to shoot the lady up with drugs. Her arm was resting on his leg. I had seen people shoot up drugs on television—but never directly in front of me. Her body was moving uncontrollably, but as the drugs entered her body, it seemed to calm her. What was also disturbing was their significant age gap. She appeared to be in her twenties, and the guy was likely in his fifties or sixties. I tried to ignore what was going on, but it was hard when it was staring me dead in the face.

I continued to walk, and I saw a group of middle-aged people on the grass. Two men and a woman were talking. One of the men was shirtless and didn't have any teeth. I sat down on the bench and placed my head in my lap to rest. I couldn't help but smell the ripeness of my own body.

"What time is Smoke barbecuing?" one of the men asked the group. "I am so damn hungry!"

"Who the hell knows! Won't you go ask him!" the lady shrieked.

They went back and forth about who was barbecuing for a good fifteen minutes.

I raised my head and scanned the area. *I don't think I will be able to fall asleep out here. I'm too paranoid, and I'm hot.*

The woman was still shaking as she and the older man disappeared into one of the abandoned homes on the street.

A blonde woman in her thirties walked up to the group sitting next to me.

The shirtless man said, "You get the smokes or what?"

She reached into the top of her shirt and then into what appeared to be her bra, pulled out two or three cigarettes, and handed them to the man.

I turned away slightly. I did not want to appear to be staring.

"Wendy, were you able to bring my beer from the tent?" the older woman barked.

"Nope, nope! I did not see it. Someone must have took it!" Wendy turned to the men and exclaimed, "You're welcome for the cigarettes!"

Both men yelled, "Thank you!"

All four of them started smoking. They all looked exhausted. Their clothes were dirty and occasionally released an unpleasant odor with the breeze. The hair of both women looked thin and brittle enough to fall out if you touched it. Both men were balding.

"Hey, man, you want a smoke?" the older woman asked me.

I was caught off guard by the offer. "Oh, no, no thank you," I answered, quickly looking over at them before turning my head away.

A man I recognized from Friday night entered the park with a grocery cart full of his belongings: blankets, a folded-up tent, clothes, and soda cans. He was missing an eye. He walked gingerly over to the water fountain and washed his hands. He could barely stand, but he was determined to wash his face with the trickle of water that was coming out.

After a few minutes, the man limped to the other side of the park.

I shifted my focus back to the four and said, "Hey, guys, how is your day going?"

They all laughed sarcastically at me—except for Wendy.

The shirtless man said, "That wasn't a serious question, was it?"

I responded, "I meant for it to be a serious question, you know, a conversation starter, but if I—"

"Does it look like we are having a good day? Look, I don't mean to bust your balls, man. We just had most of our belongings stolen out of our tent last night that we worked so hard for."

"Aw, man, I'm sorry to hear that." I felt sorry for them. *When you have very little, and it all gets taken from you, it only furthers the despair.*

"It is what it is. We are trying to figure shit out now. Hey, this is my adopted family. That's Wendy, Mary, Fred, and I am Gary." Surprisingly, they did not ask me for my name.

"Nice to meet you guys—and again, sorry about your things being stolen."

Fred said, "It's the streets. You are at everyone's mercy out here. You just got to keep rolling."

The street adjacent to the park started to come alive with people.

"I hear you on that. Say, what's going on down the street?" I asked.

Gary shouted. "Oh, that's people going to get some of Smoke's famous barbecue!"

"Who is Smokes?"

"Smokes is a friend of ours who usually barbecues every Sunday—just around the corner." Gary pointed behind him. "We usually give him a few bucks, and he hooks us up with ribs, burgers, and whatever else he gots on the grill."

Wendy said, "But sometimes he gets stingy and does not want to give us shit!"

I wanted to acknowledge Smokes's kindness, but I did not want to start an argument and left it alone.

Gary said, "You don't like him because he hardly ever gives you any food!"

Wendy said, "No! Hell no! That ain't the reason! The reason is that bastard stole my purse that day—and you all know it!"

Gary said, "If I knew—hell, if we all knew—without a doubt that he stole your purse, we would not be cool with him either! We don't have proof!"

I could tell the situation was going to escalate, and I decided to step in. "Sorry to hear that about your purse, Wendy. It sucks when our stuff gets stolen, so I understand your anger. I'm curious about something else."

Everyone stopped arguing and focused on what I was about to say.

"How do you guys know each other?" I said.

"This is my wife right here of twenty-something years." Fred kissed Mary's cheek. "We started caring for Wendy when she was way young. Her mother had actually left her in the streets, and she became, um, the daughter we never had."

Mary and Fred were teary-eyed and gave each other a hug.

Wendy came over, and all three of them hugged.

"And they made me a part of the family a few years back!" Gary said loudly. "I had just got out of prison about two years ago and ended up on the streets shortly after my release because I could not find a job. The system is jacked up, man. Nobody wanted to hire a felon, you know? So, I started smoking dope and doing what I can to survive, you know? And then God put these beautiful people in my life—and here I am now with a family I never had."

Just like in a family therapy session, I wanted to process the emotions as I normally would after a breakthrough. Reality hit, and I had to remind myself that it was not therapy—and they were not my clients. We were still in the streets, sitting at a park, in one of the most violent parts of town. Instead of responding, I just watched the family interact. They looked much happier than they had a few moments ago when they were arguing.

"Shit, the police are here!" someone yelled from the street.

I looked around, but I didn't see anyone.

"They are going to kick us out the park—same old story," Gary said. "Let's pack up our stuff and head to the tent."

"You guys have a tent?" I asked.

"Yes, um, we got an eight-person tent around the corner," Wendy said with a grin. "Do you want to stay with us?"

"I would love to, but I have to meet someone real soon." As they gathered their belongings, I started to feel sad. The small amount of time we had spent together had left an impression on me. I got up and gave them each a hug, realizing it would probably be the last time I ever saw them. I said goodbye one last time and headed out of the park to my final destination.

Seeking water at a nearby homeless shelter

NINE

The Final Two

A S I STOOD ACROSS THE STREET FROM ONE OF THE DOWNTOWN shelters, I looked up at the clock on the hotel. It was six o'clock and 103 degrees. I sat down and tried to make the time pass faster. The excitement was setting in. I was that much closer to seeing my family.

The line for folks to get a free, hot dinner was dwindling. I could smell Smokes's famous barbeque permeating the air. My appetite was resurfacing again, and I could hear my stomach growling. I couldn't think of the last time I had gone an entire day without eating anything. I decided to cross the street, which was infested with trash, to grab some water from the water cooler near the side entrance of the shelter. I hadn't had any water in about three hours, and my mouth and throat were extremely dry. I filled up my hand-sized plastic cup about six times, gulping the water down as fast as I could. Water was dripping down my chin and down my shirt.

As I sat back down on the curb and gazed out at the people, I was no longer concerned with the trash and the surrounding smells of urine inhabiting my senses. I reflected on the stories of all the people I had come across during my weekend journey. I had encountered so many distinct personalities, diverse cultural backgrounds, and heart-wrenching testimonies. Each one had been unique, but despair was the equalizer. They all felt it. In fact, I had felt it too. I could not help but think that I could have easily been one of them. If the trajectory of my life changed even slightly, it could be me sleeping in shelters or on the street corners.

I'd encountered several Shelbys, Sandys, and Bettys in my personal and professional life. They had all experienced extenuating circumstances. Many of them could have fallen victim to homelessness, but they had their families to provide a safety net that kept them from completely hitting rock bottom. Most of the people on the streets did not have a safety net available to them—or they had exhausted its intended use.

As a mental health professional observing the situation firsthand, the depths of the personal trauma I experienced was alarming. Their stories told of trauma from their past, but living on the streets brought about another level of retraumatization.

I was homeless for only forty-eight hours, and that affected my mental health in ways I would have never imagined. Depression and anxiety were two of the situational clinical presentations I was manifesting, and during my second night, I experienced some thought disturbance due to sleep deprivation. I kept seeing that man in my mind, and the countless insects I thought were crawling on me were not there. I experienced so many changes to my mental state—in such a short period of time—that I could only empathize with those who are chronically homeless. I could never fathom the level of mental health issues they have manifested, and I have no doubt that I would have met the clinical criteria for several mental health disorders if I had been in their shoes.

Living in the streets is daunting. There are serious safety concerns to be considered, adding another layer of stress to an already stressful situation. So, how does someone cope with these traumas? Alcohol, cigarettes, sex, and illicit substances appeared to be everywhere, and I lost track of the number of times I was either offered something or asked if I had any of the aforementioned items. I've never used drugs, but some of the despair I experienced—on a short-term basis—made me think about how I would cope if I did not have the hope of returning to my cushy lifestyle, the stability of my nine-to-five job, and the love and support of my family. If my predicament was a long-term one, it would have been very difficult for me to refrain from the vices that were rampant around me.

As a homeless person living in society, you are perceived as having no value. You have no home or personal effects, and you barely have enough money to buy a meal. I experienced it firsthand. There were countless people who had walked right past me as I was sprawled out on the hot concrete. They acted like I did not exist. I was invisible. I was a nobody. If I was invisible, what value did I have?

I feel it is our responsibility as human beings to be kind to everyone. If we made a point of showing a little kindness to this population, it could go a long way. It wouldn't solve homelessness, but it might provide some people with the additional support they so desperately need—and it would make them feel valued. Something as common as a smile, a genuine look of concern, and words of encouragement made a tremendous impact on my ability to survive the forty-eight hours. Watching children try to reconcile my predicament in their heads provided me with some of my greatest sense of hope because I knew that they cared. Sandy offered me water, even though she was the one suffering, and that act of kindness evoked enough compassion in me that it made me want to trade places with her. People existed and survived despite the surrounding pressures, and they were kind.

After the sun finally set, I knew I was getting close. I started to succumb to my emotions. As excited as I was to return to the normalcy of my life, I was just as sad to be leaving behind the world that I had come to respect. It embraced me for who I was and not for who I would become or for what I had to offer. I was leaving it and all the amazing people in it behind: the tears, the pain, the smiles, the friendships, the journeys, and the unknown. It almost felt like I was turning my back on them. In fact, my heart couldn't understand why our lives had to be so drastically different. The only way I could make the invisible visible and give a voice to the voiceless would be to share with the world what this world really was like.

It started getting darker, and I finally stood up to look at the clock. It was 7:49 p.m. I remained standing, preparing myself to see my family for what felt like the first time—as a person from a different world that they would never know. As I started walking back toward the park, I ran into Fred, Mary, and the rest of the family. I handed them the remaining four dollars I had in my pocket, and I wished them well.

I kept walking toward the meet-up spot, and my excitement was growing with each step. I saw my family pass by in my car, and they drove by—unaware of my presence.

ABOUT THE AUTHOR

Born and raised in Southern California, Dr. Sheldon A. Jacobs currently resides in Las Vegas, Nevada, with his beautiful wife, Nicole, his son, Jayden, and his daughter, Arianna. Dr. Jacobs has taught numerous courses at the university level and has written multiple published articles on topics ranging from mental health to various social issues. He is a licensed marriage and family therapist and an advocate for individuals who are homeless along with those suffering from mental health issues. To learn more about Dr. Jacobs, please visit his website, <u>drsheldonjacobs.com</u>

CPSIA information can be obtained
at www.ICGtesting.com
Printed in the USA
BVHW032049111120
593007BV00002B/12

9 781480 896239